THE COMPLETE GUIDE TO MAKING
LAMPSHADES

THE COMPLETE GUIDE TO MAKING
LAMPSHADES

Jane Warren

✳ THE CROWOOD PRESS

CONTENTS

INTRODUCTION

Lampshades were first created to have a practical role in our homes – to hide the glare of the light emitted from the light fittings – but they soon became a key decorative interiors item as they literally light up the design on the fabric or paper used to make them. The designs of lampshades also have to meet the need of the lighting that is required:

- ambient – the key overall lighting in the room
- task – directional lighting, for example over a kitchen work surface, or a standard lamp to aid reading
- accent – personalising your space with a particular design – statement lampshades that highlight a room's interior decor.

All these layers of lighting add to the atmosphere created in our homes. Consequently, there are many different types and styles of lampshades that are required and we often change our lampshades when we redecorate or move house.

Large commercial outlets often cannot supply us with the exact lampshade we want – in the right frame size or shape, with certain fittings, using a matching or designer fabric or adding trims to create interest, and they are often imported in mass quantities. As a result, there is a return to making our own – as with many interior and craft items, there is a surge of interest in revisiting traditional skills, combined with an increasing love of interiors fashion and style. With the advent of more people designing their own fabric, and more students graduating with degrees in surface pattern and textile design, there are more interesting and impactful designs available and therefore to choose from – they deserve to be lit up!

This book teaches you the key methods for making lampshades in many different styles – starting with the simple contemporary hard backed drum, progressing to the more complex hand sewn, including traditional tailored and gathered and pleated lampshades. You can also add your own design detail by making hand sewn trims, in your own choice of fabrics and materials, making your lampshades truly bespoke – the options are endless! Making lampshades is not a difficult process. Indeed, the simple drum takes little time and a small amount of fabric. It is not expensive and they are fun and interesting to make. To make hand sewn lampshades, you do need – or require the desire to have – a love of hand sewing; they are a slow make, taking time to stitch for a great finish.

It is always beneficial too to remake our lampshades using the original materials; with the goal of preserving both the environment and the craft, top tips are included here. Start the book by learning the basic 'how-tos', and as you progress through the tutorials, you will develop your skills to make some wonderful works of art, fashioned to your own designs.

Learning the skills of lampshade making will allow you to make unique and bespoke lighting, including recycling traditional frames and partnering them with beautiful fabrics. (Photo: Caitlin Warren)

PART 1
HARD LAMPSHADES

Hard lampshades, also known as 'card' or 'firm' lampshades, refer to the fact that the materials used to make them are rigid — usually a vinyl laminate backing onto which fabric or paper are attached. The laminate material is fire retardant, and remains so once the chosen material is adhered to it. Unlike 'soft' traditional lampshades, there is no hand sewing to make these, they are relatively inexpensive, take little time to make and a wide variety of fabrics and papers can be used to make them. They can also be made in many different shapes and sizes, including square, rectangular, oval, hexagonal as well as the classic empire and drum shapes. In addition, double-sided lampshades add extra interest with perhaps a plain linen on the outside with a vibrant patterned fabric inside. As well as the size and shape, the fabric or paper chosen is the main star of the show, with endless options giving different 'looks', from traditional to contemporary to luxury designer fabrics that really bring personality. You can also add interest with metallic liners and eye-catching and opulent trims.

As well as using available fabrics, and for something entirely unique and bespoke, lampshades can be made using your own designed fabrics or paper, using block-printing techniques or painting a plain lampshade in a chosen design (*see* Chapter 3), and by adding various trims and bindings.

AKINDE African wax print drum lampshade by Detola and Geek. Made by Tola Laseinde, whose handcrafted, African-inspired lampshades are bold, colourful and unique.

◀ Drum lampshade made using luxury velvet with gold liner made by Rab Moghal of Light Owl, bringing opulence to lighting design.

CHAPTER 1

MATERIALS AND GETTING STARTED

The materials needed to make hard lampshades can be found in a lampshade-making kit or you can buy the individual components.

Kits versus the Individual Components

There are two ways of making hard lampshades – either using a kit or using the individual components needed. The kits come with all the materials (apart from the chosen fabric or paper cover required) and are good to purchase if you wish to make one or two lampshades at a regular size, or if you are making your first hard lampshade, as the laminate panel is pre-cut for you. However, if you wish to make lampshades with different heights, or to make more of them, then it is worth buying the individual components. The instructions for both methods are included in the step-by-step instructions in Chapter 2.

Laminate Backing Panels

The laminate materials come in a wide choice of colours and finishes that show on the inside of the lampshade. Most often used is white laminate; however, clear, gold, silver and copper are very popular, as are cream and white card. Also available is eco-board, which is more environmentally friendly, and is sourced from carefully managed and renewed forests. The reverse side of the laminate is covered in a backing paper, underneath which the surface is adhesive. It is this side that the selected fabric or paper is adhered to, and will be on the outside of the lampshade.

TOOLS AND MATERIALS NEEDED TO MAKE HARD LAMPSHADES

The key tools and materials are:

- a laminate panel
- ring sets
- double-sided sticky tape
- card or roll-edged tool
- scissors
- pencil
- ruler or grid rule
- tape measure
- your choice of fabric or paper.

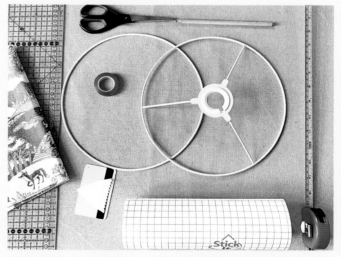

Gather together the tools and materials needed to make hard lampshades.

The laminate used to create hard lampshades can be cut to the size and shape needed.

There is a large choice of lining backing materials to make lampshades – from white to neon PVC to cream card. Stick-It ® materials manufactured by Dannells.

Hard Lampshades and Fire Retardancy

All laminate materials made for hard lampshades have been tested in the Lighting Association Laboratories and have passed the glow wire test. Fabrics and papers that are adhered to the laminate materials are therefore fire resistant – even those adhered to the inside of the lampshades, as in the double-sided laminate. However, always use LED bulbs, which are cool to the touch, and will help prevent any scorching to the inside of the lampshade.

Ring Sets and Fittings

Hard lampshades have two wire rings that are needed for the structure of the lampshade. One ring is plain, and the other is a 'utility' ring. This ring holds the light fitting used to connect the lampshade to the lamp holder – either on a lampbase or on a ceiling/pendant – using 'gimbals' (the metal arms that connect the light fitting to the ring). The laminate backing with your chosen fabric is then adhered to the rings to make the lampshade, with the following choices of utility rings.

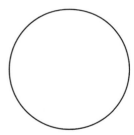

A plain ring is paired with a utility ring that holds the light fitting to create the lampshade.

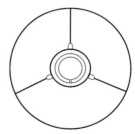

A utility ring holds the light fitting, as well as a removeable adaptor to suit both EU and UK lamp holders.

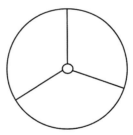

A US washer ring is for use with a harp and finial fitting, most commonly used in the USA, and is just 10mm (⅓in) wide.

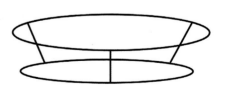

A duplex ring/fitting is positioned in a top ring and allows the lampshade to be used both for lamp bases and as ceiling fittings.

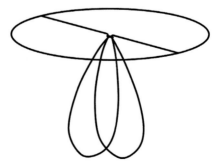

Candle clips are fixed to the top ring and fit neatly onto a candle or small golf-ball bulb.

A drop-down fitting is attached to the top ring but 'dropped down' to the middle of the lampshade by long gimbals (the metal arms that attach a light fitting to a ring).

Plain Rings

Plain rings are paired with a choice of utility rings to make hard lampshades in all shapes and sizes.

Standard Utility Rings

Standard utility rings are manufactured to fit European lamp holders, and an adaptor plug is fitted to reduce the diameter so that it can fit standard UK lamp holders (bayonet cap B22). This can easily be removed to fit European lamp holders (Edison screw E27).

Washer Fittings

Some lampshades have a washer fitting for use with a harp and finial, most commonly used in the USA, the opening of which is just 10mm diameter. You can also purchase converters so that your EU/UK standard fitting can be converted to use as a harp and finial lamp holder.

Duplex Fittings

A duplex fitting is a large ring positioned within the top ring. It offers flexibility for your lampshade, by either being used for a lamp base or standard lamp (you will need a shade carrier for this) or as a ceiling/pendant shade (you will need a spider fitting for this). Shade carriers come in a variety of heights, from 10cm to 30cm. Spider fittings come in an EU size with a UK converter. Therefore you can make a lampshade with a duplex fitting to give you full flexibility should you wish to. They are also chosen because the standard utility ring's light fitting is positioned 4cm above the base ring, and this may mean the lampshade is too low for the lamp base.

Candle Clip Fittings

Candle clip fittings are attached to the top ring of small lampshades, usually made for wall lights or chandeliers, and neatly fit onto a candle or small golf-ball bulb.

Drop-Down Fittings

A drop-down fitting is where the light fitting is attached to the top ring but is 'dropped down' to the middle of the lampshade by long gimbals. These are particularly useful if making lampshades that require a top ring only, such as scallop or paper pleated lampshades. Some drop-down fittings have hinges so that the lampshade can be tilted (for reading) or for allowing the lampshade to work for a ceiling pendant fitting.

Shade carriers fit onto table or standard lamps by being placed onto the lamp holder fitted to the base. The lampshade is then simply placed onto the top of the shade carrier. As mentioned, they come in a variety of heights, from 10cm to 30cm. This is useful as you can then choose one that suits the lamp base perfectly. If it is too low it may hide some of the lamp base design; if it is too high it will reveal the metal or plastic lamp holder and bulb. In addition, having a shade carrier makes it easy to clean your lampshade as it can be simply lifted off the base. Having a duplex fitting in your lampshade offers flexibility as it can also be used as a pendant lampshade – simply add a spider fitting to a ceiling fitting and place the shade onto that.

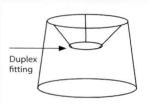

Duplex fitting

The duplex fitting is placed in the top ring of the lampshade, ready for either a shade carrier or a spider fitting.

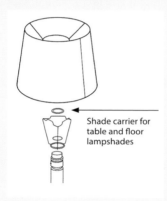

Shade carrier for table and floor lampshades

A shade carrier is fixed onto a lamp base, and the lampshade is placed on top of this.

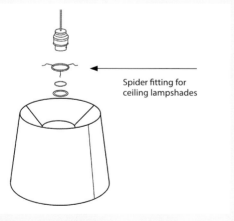

Spider fitting for ceiling lampshades

By using a spider fitting, the lampshade can be connected to a ceiling light fitting to become a pendant lampshade.

Diffusers

A diffuser is used to soften the light that comes into the room, to hide the inside of the lampshade, and for decoration. They are therefore mainly used with ceiling lampshades and focus the eye on the design of the outside. The diffuser is a disc the size of the circumference of the base lampshade ring. They come in a variety of styles, from translucent to featuring cut-out designs. In addition you can adhere your choice of fabric onto these (*see* Suppliers), offering a totally bespoke lighting option. They are installed by simply placing them at an angle, and then straightened to sit in the base ring.

Tube Lights by The Bespoke Boutique in collaboration with Eva Sonaike for C.P. Hart.

SIZES AND SHAPES OF HARD LAMPSHADES

There are many different shapes of hard lampshade to choose to make:

- drum lampshade – the top and base rings are the same size
- empire – the top ring is half the size of the base ring
- French drum – the top ring is smaller than the base ring, as in the empire, but less so
- cone or coolie shape – the top ring is far smaller than the base ring
- oval – the top and base rings are oval – much wider than the depth
- rectangular and square
- hexagonal
- tiered shades
- half frames, wall lights.

The rings and ring sets you can buy now mostly come in increments of 5cm, ranging from 10cm to 100cm. However, you can get different sizes made to order by commissioning a frame maker or by remaking older hard lampshades (*see* Chapter 3 for remaking hard lampshades).

Laminate Panel Lengths for Drums

If a lampshade-making kit is being used, the laminate panel will be pre-cut with a determined height. If you are using all the individual materials, however, the panel will need to be cut from a roll of laminate.

First work out the amount of laminate needed to fit around the ring sets, plus allow an extra 15mm minimum for the seam allowance. For example:

- You can calculate that a 30cm diameter drum will have a circumference of 94.2cm (diameter × pi (or 3.14)) + 15mm seam = 95.7, rounded up to 96cm.
- You then need to decide on the height of the lampshade.
- Using a rule, draw these measurements onto the paper-covered side of the laminate and use scissors or a knife to carefully cut it out, taking time to be accurate.

DESIGNS AND SUGGESTED SIZES OF HARD LAMPSHADES

In a lampshade making kit, the sizes have already been decided. However, you may wish to make some with different dimensions. The laminate panel can be cut to have different heights for drum lampshades, but for other shapes they should be in proportion. The table offers suggested sizes; however, you can create your own templates and choices.

SUGGESTED SIZES FOR HARD LAMPSHADES

Drum	Empire	French drum	Cone
Drums have the same size top and base rings	Empires have a base ring that is twice the diameter of the top ring	The French drum is an empire but there is less difference in size between the rings	The cone has a much smaller top ring than the base ring
Size: Little 15cm rings Height: 15cm	Little: 10cm top ring 20cm base ring Height: 14.5cm	Little: 10cm top ring 15cm base ring Height: 15cm	
Size: Small 20cm rings Height: 18cm	Small: 15cm top ring 25cm base ring Height: 17cm	Small: 15cm top ring 20cm base ring Height: 16.5cm	Small: 10cm top ring 25cm base ring Height: 16cm
Size: Medium 25cm rings Height: 21cm	Medium: 15cm top ring 30cm base ring Height: 20cm	Medium: 25cm top ring 30cm base ring Height: 19cm	Medium: 15cm top ring 40cm base ring Height: 20cm
Size: Medium + 30cm rings Height: 22cm	Medium +: 20cm top ring 35cm base ring Height: 25cm	Medium +: 30cm top ring 35cm base ring Height: 25cm	Medium +: 20cm top ring 45cm base ring Height: 25cm
Size: Large 40cm rings Height: 25cm	Large: 20cm top ring 40cm base ring Height: 27cm	Large: 35cm top ring 40cm base ring Height: 27cm	Large: 20cm top ring 50cm base ring Height: 45cm

Notes: These are suggested sizes only – bespoke designs and sizes can be created by making or purchasing a template (*see* 'Templates for Hard Lampshades' later in this chapter). Imperial size rings are also available in sizes: 8in, 10in, 12in, 14in, 16in and 18in.

The fabric requirement will be the same as the panel, plus some extra to gain neat edges and for tucking under the rings (*see* tuition in Chapter 2) – allow some extra all the way around. The table shows the sizes of materials needed, when not using a kit, for drum shades:

HOW MUCH LAMINATE AND FABRIC TO CUT FOR NON-KIT DRUM SHADES

Drum lampshade size (diameter)	Panel length to cut (including 15mm seam)	Fabric length (minimum)
15cm	49cm	53cm
20cm	64.5cm	69cm
25cm	80cm	84cm
30cm	96cm	100cm
35cm	111.5cm	115cm
40cm	127.5cm	132cm
45cm	143cm	147cm
50cm	159cm	163cm
55cm	174.5cm	179cm
60cm	190.5cm	194cm
70cm	222cm	226cm

Notes: Figures have been rounded up for ease.

Choose the height of the shade for non-kit lampshades, just cut the panel to the required height, plus allow around 4cm extra fabric for the height.

Lampshades over 40cm will usually need to have fabric either turned sideways (railroaded) or joined with an extra seam positioned opposite the main seam (*see* Chapter 3 for tuition).

How Much Fabric Is Needed for Empire Lampshades?

Empire, French drum, and cone lampshades have curved panels, and therefore the fabric requirements are different from the drum lampshades. The empire and cone lampshade-making kits advise how much fabric is needed to cover the area of the laminate panel. When using a template and using the individual components required, however, the following guide advises how much fabric will be needed for a few examples of empire-shaped lampshades.

AREA OF FABRIC NEEDED FOR EMPIRE SHADES

Empire size	Height (slope)	Fabric width/length	Fabric height
10cm top 20cm base	14.5cm	60cm	35cm
15cm top 25cm base	17cm	75cm	35cm
15cm top 30cm base	20cm	85cm	38cm
20cm top 40cm base	27cm	120cm	50cm

Notes: Figures given are the minimum fabric area needed to cover your laminate panel.

Lampshade sizes are suggestions only.

Templates for Hard Lampshades

Creating and cutting a laminate panel to the correct size for drum lampshades is a straightforward process. However, to make empire, French drum, or cone-shaped lampshades, a templated laminate panel is required for this as they are curved. There are various ways of achieving this:

- Purchase a kit with a ready-cut laminate panel to use.
- Arrange for a bespoke templated panel to be made by visiting the website of the lampshade materials manufacturer who offers this service and ordering a bespoke size (*see* Suppliers on page 172).
- Similarly, the supplier offers the option to use a tool on their website to download a template that you can then print at home.
- Work out a template or pattern at home.

In all cases, once the lampshade has been made, the backing paper of the laminate panel can be kept as a pattern to use should you wish to make more of that lampshade size in the future.

MAKING A TEMPLATE OR PATTERN YOURSELF

You can work out the drawing for a template by following these steps and using these tools and materials:

- large piece of paper or card
- pencil
- string or waxed jewellery cord
- pin
- set square and rule
- tape measure

Decide on the dimensions of the lampshade you wish to make, and make a note of them, for example:

- base 25cm diameter
- top 15cm diameter
- height 17cm (note this is the vertical height; the slope height will be slightly longer)

Work out the circumferences (diameter × pi (3.14)). For the above example, the base would be 25 × 3.14 = 78.5cm and the top would be 15 × 3.14 = 47.1cm.

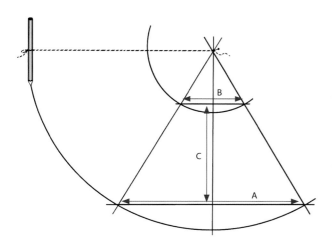

Use the template pattern maker at home to create various sizes for your lampshades.

Follow these steps to make the template:

1. Lay the card or paper on a table, and in the right-hand base of it draw a horizontal line the measurement of the base ring diameter (line A).

2. Find the centre point of this line and draw a vertical line upwards from that point, the height of the lampshade (line C). Use a set square for precision.

3. Now draw a horizontal line the measurement of the top diameter of the lampshade (line B). This should be centred above line A.

4. Draw lines upwards from the ends of lines A, B, and C, to where they connect, which will make a triangle. Make a mark at this key point.

5. Put a pin in this key point, attach a piece of string or cord (waxed, thin jewellery cord is best as it doesn't stretch) to it, and attach the other end of this to a pencil.

6. Position the pencil exactly at the right-hand point of line A, and draw the arc around, as long as the measurement of the circumference plus 15mm for a seam allowance. You can mark the circumference by making small measurements around the curve, placing small pencil marks for accuracy – use a measure and place a mark every 1cm, so that it is exact.

7. Then attach the pencil to the cord so that it is positioned to the right edge of line B and draw another curve, again taking care to get the circumference measurement exactly right, adding on the 15mm seam allowance.

8. Draw a line connecting the two ends of the curves (which should include the 15mm seam allowance).

9. Cut out the template carefully all around. Place it on top of some laminate and draw around this. It helps to weigh it down for accuracy; use a pencil or knife to cut out and make your lampshade.

FABRICS AND PAPERS TO USE

There is a huge amount of fabrics and papers available to choose from, both from shops, fabric suppliers, and online.

Fabrics

As a rule, the easiest fabrics to work with are medium-weight cottons or cotton mixes, as they are happy to be adhered to the laminate panel, don't fray particularly, and don't pucker or shift when you make the lampshade; in other words, they behave well. The weave is important to consider, as loose weaves may mean the laminate might be visible, and the fabric could shift when using it. Other materials to use are hessian (made from jute), raffia (a thicker weave than hessian), and parchment (traditionally made from animal skin, now available using a thin translucent paper). Obtain samples first and adhere them to a piece of the laminate to check they will work and stay stuck down in advance of making the lampshade.

Tips on Using Different Fabrics

Wool: Ensure a little more fabric is cut along the horizontal edges, as they are thicker to fold under the rings.

Velvet: As with wool; with both wool and velvet, it may help to hand sew down the seam once you have made the lampshade, to keep the seam closed (*see* Chapter 3 for tips and Chapter 4 for sewing tuition).

Silk: This has a tendency to pop away from the laminate panel, as it notoriously doesn't like being stuck down. However, try small samples of different types on samples of laminate to check if it will stay in place before making the lampshade, as some may be successful. Faux silks are perfect for hard lampshades as the synthetic material happily adheres to the laminates.

Thin fabrics: Take extra care to ensure the fabric stays straight when you adhere it to the panel; it can move or 'shift' around and can easily pucker. Taking your time and re-doing it if necessary will help.

Calico: This can pop away from the laminate after the shade has been made. Wash in advance to help with this.

Embroidered fabrics: Although it is possible to use these, bear in mind that the area around the embroidered part may lift away from the laminate, as it is thicker than the base cloth used.

Working with Papers

As well as using fabrics, papers can also be used to produce wonderful hard lampshades. There are a variety of types to use, including Japanese *washi* paper, hand-marbled papers, wallpapers, and even gift wrap. They easily adhere to the laminate but are often not wide enough to cover the whole length of your laminate panel, and therefore widths of the paper are used to fit. In this case, it is important to pattern match the design, so consider this when you choose your paper and how much you will need (*see* how to join fabric and papers for larger shades in Chapter 3). Consider also using a cream card laminate as the backing; because it is thicker, the design on the paper is more pronounced when the lampshade is lit.

This hand-marbled paper by Rachel Maiden for Maiden Marbling was used to make this stand-out drum lampshade. Made by Jane Warren.

Designs and Patterns to Consider for Hard Lampshades

When choosing patterned fabrics or papers to make hard lampshades, it is worth being mindful of the following design tips:

- For empire lampshades, the panel will be curved but the pattern will not be. It is therefore better to use a fabric or paper with a small pattern repeat.
- Large patterns may not fit in the confines of the laminate panel, so use them only for larger shades.
- If a lampshade-making kit is being used, it will have a defined height. Therefore it is worth considering where the elements of your design may lie – it is best to avoid large blank spaces or a feature cut in half, for example.
- As the length of the laminate panel cannot be changed, it is not possible to pattern match your fabric or paper at the seam; check the placement before making to get the best result.

See more information and practical tips on pattern placement in Chapter 2.

Trims and Bindings for Hard Lampshades

Trims can easily be attached to the outside of hard lampshades by simply placing double-sided sticky tape or glue around the edge of the base and top of the lampshade, and adhering the chosen trim. Bias binding can be made or purchased to add a complementary or pop of colour too; it is also widely used to make lampshades using paper, because often the paper puckers as it is folded over the rings. There are instructions for making bias binding in Chapter 8 and how to adhere it in Chapter 2.

When working with papers, it is best to use the thicker card laminate backing so that the design stands out. Paper by Cambridge Imprint, in various colourways of their 'Milky Way' design.

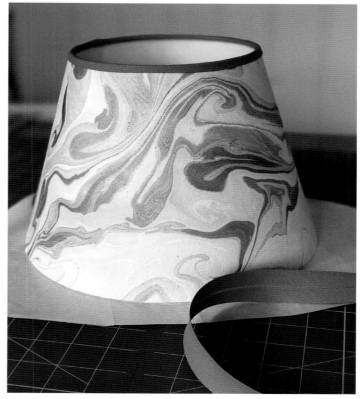

Bias binding is often attached to hard lampshades as a trim, to complete a design and particularly for those made using paper.

CHAPTER 2

MAKING HARD LAMPSHADES

THE CLASSIC DRUM AND EMPIRE

Drum lampshades have the same size top and base rings, and empires have a larger base ring than top ring, but both are made using the same methods.

Getting Started

Before starting to make a lampshade, it is good working practice to put together the equipment and materials needed in advance so they are all to hand:

- table – a long table that is 500cm minimum deep, and which should be clean and free of clutter
- self-healing cutting mat – this is useful to have on the table because they offer perfect protection for tables as well as making it easier to cut the fabric and laminates, especially if using a knife or rotary cutter; plus they have marked measurements and angles
- ironing board and iron – it is imperative that the fabric is ironed really smooth, as any wrinkles or creases will show up on the lampshade, especially when lit
- a lampshade-making kit, and extra materials (or if not using a lampshade-making kit, the correct length of laminate, ring sets, and extra tools and materials, as outlined in Chapter 1)
- an item to help weigh down the panel as you make the lampshade – anything from a tin of beans to an old iron weight
- your choice of fabric or paper to make the lampshade.

A selection of St Jude's Fabrics drum and empire lampshades, expertly made by Karen Revill of Revill, Revill Lampshades.

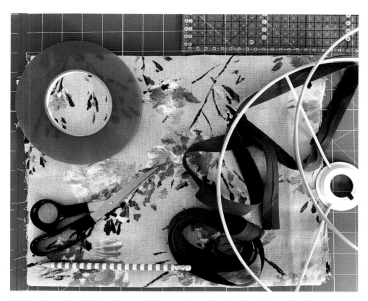

Gather together the tools needed to make a classic drum lampshade on a large clean table.

Preparing the Laminate Panel Included in the Kit

The lampshade panel will be rolled up very tight in the kit box, and if used straight after unrolling it, may result in having a wavy lampshade. Take it out of the box, unroll it, and lay it flat, placing heavy books or other weights on it for a few days until it is totally flat and ready to use.

Making Drum Lampshades

Drum hard lampshades are perhaps the most straightforward to make, and therefore are a good choice for a first lampshade, especially if using a lampshade-making kit. Because the rings are the same size, it is easier to both adhere your fabric for pattern placement and to roll the ring sets onto the laminate panel.

Pattern Placement

It is worth spending time considering the pattern on your chosen fabric. Using a kit means that the finished lampshade will not be as tall as the laminate panel supplied. This is because there are scored edges (sometimes known as 'kiss cuts') along the lengths both top and base; these edges are 15mm in height and will be removed to leave some fabric to be tucked under the rings, meaning the finished lampshade will be 3cm less tall. As an example, the 25cm diameter drum lampshade that will be used in the tutorial has a laminate panel height of 24cm, but will in fact end up being 21cm. Therefore there is little point in using a design with a large dog that stands 25cm high, for example, as either its feet or head will be partly cut off.

Seam Pattern Placement

In addition, be mindful of what will appear at the seam. It is very unlikely that you can pattern match here, as the panel has a fixed length to fit around the circumference of the ring set. Although with checks and stripes there will not be a problem, there can be with patterns. For this reason, move the panel along the width of the fabric to see which position works best at the seam (ensuring you allow for the 15mm seam allowance). However, it does work out by chance from time to time, if very lucky!

Perfectly Straight Patterns

In order to guarantee that the pattern on the fabric runs straight along the top of the finished lampshade, it helps to place pins along the horizontal pattern repeat face up. This is because, when making the lampshade, the fabric is placed face down onto the table, and therefore the pattern may not be visible. Adding these pins will ensure a straight line.

Planning Your Pattern Layout

Because of the fixed height of the lampshade panel in the kit, plan for a balanced pattern placement – perhaps choose a feature to put in the middle. Use a ruler to pinpoint the centre of the panel and then the centre of the pattern on the fabric. Place a pencil mark on the laminate edge and a pin in the fabric. These points can then be married to ensure the perfect central positioning of your design.

Drum hard shades are perhaps the most straightforward lampshade to make, and you can add trims and use different colour linings for interest and variety.

Fabrics with a defined pattern rarely match at the seam due to lampshades having a fixed circumference and panel length – this example was a lucky result! Lampshade by Jane Warren.

Find a pattern repeat across the fabric and place pins in the repeats. This will ensure the pattern runs straight across the lampshade.

Plan your pattern layout: measure the height of the laminate panel and find the centre point; then match it with the centre of the fabric design for symmetry.

Having flattened the laminate panel and planned the fabric layout, follow these step-by-step instructions to make a drum lampshade. A 25cm drum kit has been used in this tutorial.

The completed drum lampshade, with the pattern placement planned in advance.

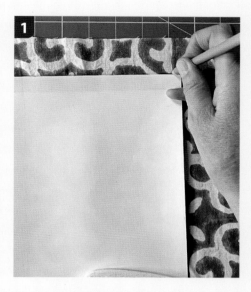

Cut the fabric 5cm larger than the panel, iron it well, and lay it face down on the table. Place the laminate panel on top (with the paper side underneath) in position, taking note of pins if used for pattern placement. Draw short lines (key lines) with pencil or chalk on the fabric, right up against the panel edge, all around.

Starting at one end of the laminate (it does not matter whether it is the left or right end), peel away around 10cm of the laminate's backing paper, and fold it underneath the panel. Ensure there are no loose threads of fabric between the sticky panel and the underside of the fabric. Now stick it down accurately in the key lines drawn. Check the front to ensure there are no wrinkles.

Continued on the following page.

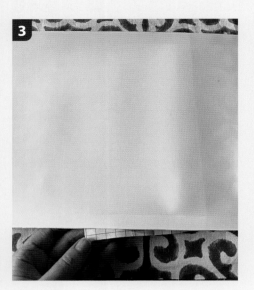

Now work along the panel length using the following four key steps. 1. Take hold of the backing paper, and pull away the next 10cm of the paper to reveal more of the sticky side. 2. Check that the panel is in the right position in the pencil key lines. 3. Smooth it onto the fabric underneath. 4. Check the front to see if it is adhering with no loose threads or wrinkles in the fabric.

To achieve a neat seam (and to avoid a cut raw edge), draw a 1cm vertical line down one end of the fabric using a grid rule or ruler. Also add extra fabric tabs at the top of the 1cm cut fabric – 1.5cm high and 1.5cm across the panel. Add a strip of double-sided tape onto this extra fabric – from the base of the scored points, not the current height of the laminate panel.

Cut away the excess fabric around the panel, except the extra 1cm edge and tabs – start there first. Carefully remove the scored strips of laminate. It is key that these are removed gently, by pushing the laminate downwards along the scores, with the panel flat on the table; otherwise it can get damaged. Remove spare threads as the strips are removed.

Remove the pink cover of double-sided tape (DST) on the 1cm fabric strip, then fold it onto the laminate. Add another piece of the DST to the other end, but on the fabric side. Do not remove the pink cover yet. Cover the rings with DST, in the middle of the rings, let it meet at the end (not overlap). Smooth it down firmly. Take off the cover, starting with the utility ring – you can stand this up while removing the tape off the plain ring.

7

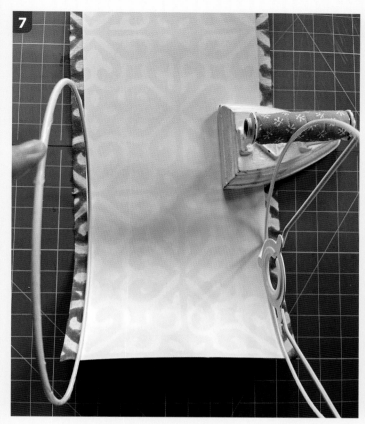

Lay the panel fabric-side down, with the extra folded end at the far end. Decide if the lampshade is to be for a ceiling (position the utility ring at the top of the panel) or a lamp base (place the utility ring at the base of the panel). Position yourself in front of the panel and the rings on the edge of the laminate; place them so that the gimbals are not by the front edge.

8

Roll the rings forward slowly. It is key not to have the rings either on the fabric or with the laminate edge showing. It can help to move one ring a few centimetres first and then the second, and repeat. It can help to turn the panel round towards you for accuracy once you get started. Once the panel has been completely rolled onto the rings, check there is no laminate sticking proud of the rings; unstick and re-roll if there is. Place the lampshade on its side, and smooth down the fabric around the rings.

On top of the gimbals, place scissors under the fabric and snip to the edge, not the top, of the ring. Now push the excess fabric under the rings: pull it up and over, and select either the tool in the kit or an old store card or small rounded-end knife to push the fabric under; position the tool onto the edge of the fabric and push it under – be firm. Leave the seam area until the end, otherwise it may result in a bowed-in seam.

9

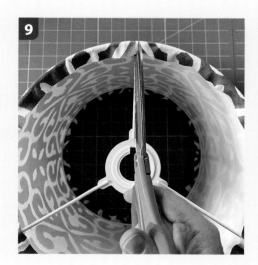

Close the seam area by removing the cover of the DST, placing the seam of the lampshade on the table, and pressing it firmly together. The tabs are needed as there is so much fabric to tuck in around the seam, especially if using a thick fabric. Trim away as much of the tab as needed, then carefully pull up and tuck under the ring.

10

Using Separate Components to Make a Drum Lampshade

The advantages of not using a kit include:

- the lampshade can be made as tall as required
- a complete pattern in the fabric design can be included
- the ability to remake lampshades using new cut-to-size laminate (*see* Chapter 3 for the remaking tutorial)
- being more cost effective – if you wish to make a few lampshades, work out the savings if you purchase the separate components.

When making a hard lampshade using separate components rather than a kit, the laminate will be delivered in a roll. Cut it down to the size required for the lampshade (*see* the 'How Much Laminate and Fabric to Cut for Non-Kit Drum Shades' table in Chapter 1 for measurements). There will not be scored cuts; therefore once you have adhered the fabric to the laminate panel, simply create the horizontal lengths of fabric needed to fold under the rings, by adding 15mm of fabric above the laminate panel along the top and base. Remember to add the tabs and the extra 1cm side edge for the neat folded seam down one end before cutting out.

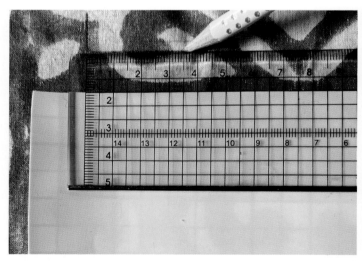

Cutting the laminate off a roll to the required size means there will not be scored 'kiss' cuts. Use a ruler and draw 15mm lines on the fabric above and below the horizontal lengths of the panel, as well as tabs and 1cm extra at one end.

Using individual lampshade making components means the laminate panel can be cut to create differently sized lampshades from those in the kits. This tall lampshade has been expertly made by Jan Hartley from Mono Handmade, ensuring the whole pattern has been included and placed centrally.

Making Empire Lampshades

Empire, French drum, and cone lampshades have smaller top rings than base rings and so must have a curved laminate panel to fit around and attach to the two rings. To make these lampshades, follow exactly the same steps and method as for making the drum; however, when attaching the rings to the laminate, slant the rings sideways a little when you roll them, so as to follow the cut edges of the laminate panel.

Pattern Placement

Using a fabric with a horizontal pattern on an empire, French drum or cone-shaped hard lampshade will present a problem in pattern placement.

The design will only appear straight at the front of the lampshade if it is placed in the middle, but as the panel is curved, the pattern will curve away too, and at the back, the horizontal detail will actually be vertical. Therefore it helps to use plain fabrics or patterns with very small designs where the change is less noticeable.

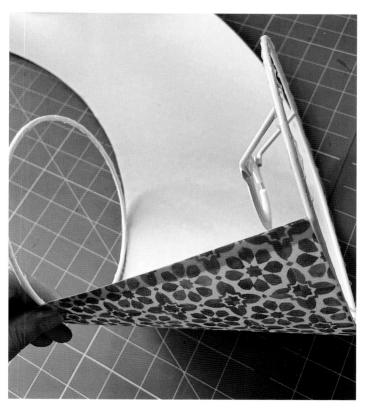

Because empire lampshades have a smaller top ring than base ring, the panel is curved. Using the same making methods as for a drum, simply hold the rings at the angle of the panel, and roll onto the laminate.

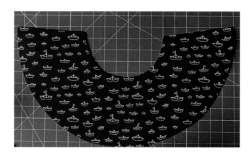

Flat panel: here the fabric has been attached to the panel. The pattern is straight but the panel is curved.

Front of lampshade: at the front, the design will look correct, as it has been made placing the straight pattern design in the middle of the lampshade panel.

Back of lampshade: because the panel is curved to fit around a smaller top than base ring, the fabric pattern will curve away as well – at the back, the design is vertical and not horizontal.

Working with Paper

There are lovely papers available to use to make lampshades, including maps, gift wrap, wallpaper, hand-marbled, Japanese *washi* and block-printed papers. Consider the size and weight of the paper, and try small samples of your papers on cut-offs of the various laminates available, seeing which work best together.

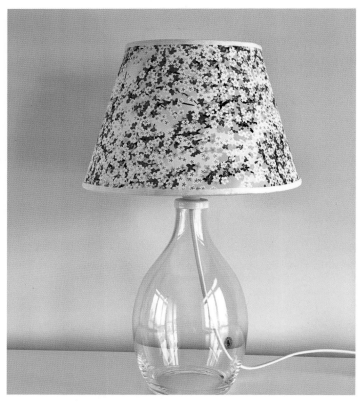

Decorative papers can be used to make lampshades of distinction. This Japanese *yuzen washi* paper is beautiful when lit, with its gold detail on a classic cherry blossom design. Paper by Lavender Home. Lampshade by Jane Warren.

This large lampshade was made for Claudine Purnell's library room, using Penguin Library Wallpaper by Osborne & Little to match. The wallpaper is 52cm wide, and therefore widths were joined to fit the length needed. Lampshade made by Jane Warren.

Paper Sizes for Lampshades

Papers can be narrow. Wallpapers, for example, are usually around 52cm wide. This means that they would fit perfectly around a small 15cm drum laminate panel (*see* the 'How Much Laminate and Fabric to Cut for Non-Kit Drum Shades' table in Chapter 1). However, if the paper is railroaded (that is, laid on its side), the height can be used as the width, pattern permitting. Other papers may come in larger sizes, such as maps, and you can also purchase extra-large pieces of Japanese *washi* paper online or order bespoke large pieces from marblers (*see* Suppliers), art shops or specialist paper producers.

Alternatively, it is possible to join papers, enabling them to fit around larger-sized lampshades (*see* 'The Oversized Lampshade' section in Chapter 3 for detail and tuition).

Making a Lampshade Using Paper with a Bias Trim

You can make this lampshade following the same method as for making the drum lampshade. However, you can also follow a different process if the paper is very thin and fragile: simply place the laminate on the table (paper side up this time), put your choice of paper on top of it, pattern side up, and adhere it this way, slowly but surely. This process gives you more control over the sticking down; using an old credit or store card will help with smoothing it down. With fabric, you can peel it away and restart if there is an error or wrinkle, but this is impossible with paper – once it is stuck, it is final!

For these lampshades, the paper is trimmed away to the edge of the laminate panel, and then a bias trim will be added. There are two reasons for this:

- some paper can pucker as it is pulled over and under the rings
- the lampshades can look far better having a block of colour as a decorative detail.

There are many choices of bias binding to purchase in shops or online, and it is straightforward to make it (follow the steps in Chapter 8 to make your own).

The lampshade in the following tutorial has been made using paper and then an added 15mm bias binding around the top and base rings.

The completed lampshade – follow the steps in the tutorial to perfect making a hard lampshade using paper with bias binding trim. Paper by Wanderlust Paper Co.

Once the lampshade has been made, and starting at the seam, put strips of 6mm double-sided tape around the base and top edges. Line up the top of the tape with the top of the ring. This will ensure the tape is the same depth all the way around.

Cut lengths of bias binding (15mm width used here) – the circumference of the rings plus a 2cm seam allowance. Open out the long edge of one side and iron it smooth. At one end of the bias, open up a little of the still folded edge and turn in around 5mm of the cut end of the bias tape. Then fold back into position the base piece so that a pocket is created.

Take the cover off the double-sided tape around the base, and adhere this folded end of the bias at the seam edge. Smooth all around the base, slightly pulling as you go for a snug fit, keeping the base of the bias in line with the base of the double-sided tape. Take your time to get this right, as the paper will pull away if re-sticking is needed.

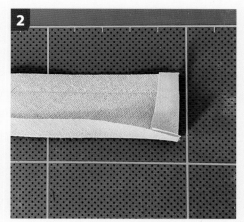

Continued on the following page.

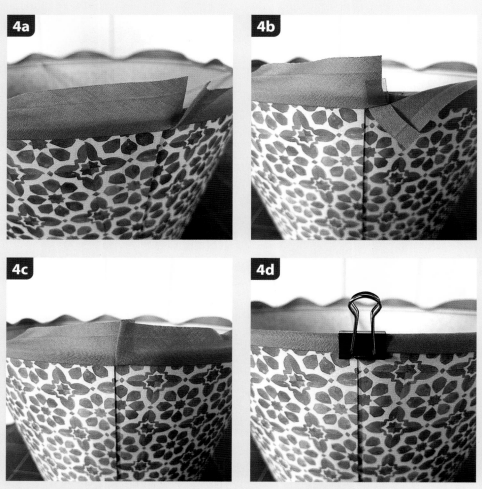

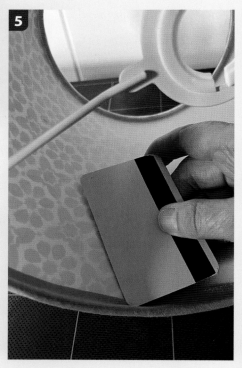

When you reach the end, trim away any excess apart from 5mm; tuck this into the pocket formed at the start. It helps to add a very small piece of double-sided sticky tape between the two pieces to attach them, plus a small bulldog clip. This ensures that the seam area of the bias does not get pulled upwards when tucking in.

Hold the opened end of the bias, and pull up and over the ring, tucking it in using the technique outlined in step 9 of the main method of making fabric lampshades. Make snips into the bias at the gimbals so it can go either side and be tucked under. Repeat for the top ring.

HINTS AND TIPS FOR MAKING PAPER LAMPSHADES

- If using a map or other printed paper for the lampshade, note that if it has text on the reverse side, it will show through when lit.
- Use a thicker laminate backing than the standard one; because paper is much thinner than fabric, the pattern on paper tends to fade away when lit.
- With hand-marbled papers, there can be spots of paint on the back of the paper – a thicker laminate will hide these.
- If using hand-marbled papers, the paint can sometimes come off onto your hands when you are attaching and smoothing down the laminate – remember to wash your hands as soon as you have finished.

- Because the paper will be adhered to the laminate, unlike with fabric, it will not be possible to pull it off and remake it – be sure of the placement before starting!
- When tucking the bias binding under the rings, where snips are needed so that it fits around the gimbals, add Fray Stop first, then snip when set – this will mean there is no fraying.
- Sometimes bias binding can be thin, and can pucker around the top edges of the rings when it is being pulled over. To remedy this, add a little cotton wool all around the top of the rings (it will stick onto the double-sided tape), then push the bias under the rings; it will create a lovely rounded edge.

Double-Sided Lampshades

It is also possible to make hard lampshades that are 'double sided' – where they have fabric or paper adhered to both the inside as well as the outside. These can bring really eye-catching extra detail to lighting and are perfect for high ceilings or hallways; having a decorative feature inside is much more interesting to peer up into than a plain white interior. Likewise, with a lampshade based on a low table, you could have a colourful interior to look into.

Making a Double-Sided Lampshade

Before making a double-sided lampshade:

- Test out the chosen fabric or paper for the inside of the lampshade by attaching a sample of it onto a sample of the laminate, and curving it round to check if the material will pop or pull away.
- Test out the two materials chosen by adhering a sample of each onto a sample of the double-sided laminate, and then holding this up to a bulb to see if the patterns match or clash.

Double-sided lampshades also bring interest if the lamp is situated on a low table in a room.

Double-sided lampshades: why look up into a white space when you can look up into historical London?

It gives a different atmosphere when lit up, too: inner wallpaper 'London 1832' by Zoffany; lampshade made by Jane Warren for The Curtain Co.

- If making a very large lampshade that is double-sided, using thickish fabrics, the lampshade may end up being very heavy. Make sure the ceiling fitting you have in place is adequate for this weight in advance!

The following tutorial is based on using individual components, not a kit.

In preparation:

1. Cut the double-sided laminate panel the correct size to make the lampshade (*see* the 'How Much Laminate and Fabric to Cut for Non-Kit Drum Shades' table in Chapter 1 for width measurements; the height is personal choice).
2. Cut out the covering for the lining (or inside) of the lampshade, allowing a little extra all around the panel.
3. Now cut the fabric or paper for the outside of the lampshade, allowing about 5cm (2in) extra all around the laminate.

TUTORIAL: MAKING A DOUBLE-SIDED LAMPSHADE

The completed double-sided lampshade, using velvet on the outside and a botanical print inside.

When the lampshade is lit, the full effect of having a highly decorative design inside is displayed.

1

First make the inside (or lining) of the lampshade – place the flattened laminate on the table, then put the selected paper or (ironed) fabric face up on top. Weigh the paper or fabric down in position. Then hold the edge of the laminate paper underneath, pulling away a few centimetres, folding the paper cover underneath the material on top. Press and smooth down.

2

Continue pulling away paper and adhering the top cover all along the length of the panel. At the end, use scissors to trim away excess fabric or paper all around. This is now the inside of the lampshade. Make the outside of the lampshade using the same method as in the 'Making Drum Lampshades' tutorial, with the extra instruction on not using a kit.

3

Add an extra 15mm of fabric to each horizontal edge, plus extra along one vertical edge with tabs, for a neat, not a raw, edge. Now roll the rings onto the panel, and make as the 'Making Drum Lampshades' tuition. If using velvet or wool to make the lampshade, it is useful to slip stitch the outside of the seam for extra strength (*see* Chapter 3 for how to do this).

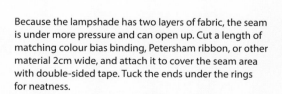

4

Because the lampshade has two layers of fabric, the seam is under more pressure and can open up. Cut a length of matching colour bias binding, Petersham ribbon, or other material 2cm wide, and attach it to cover the seam area with double-sided tape. Tuck the ends under the rings for neatness.

DIFFERENT SHAPED HARD LAMPSHADES

Square navy blue lampshades with gold linings made by Candice Small of Candid Owl, who makes lampshades in a wide variety of shapes and sizes.

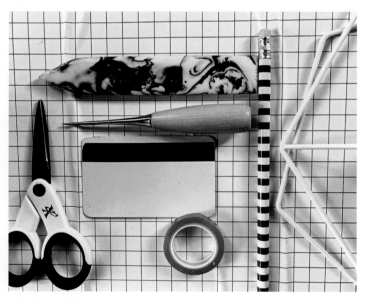

Add a bone folder (top) and scorer (underneath) to the kit needed – using them will result in good crisp edges for straight-sided hard lampshades.

As well as drum and empire shapes, hard lampshades can be made in many different sizes and shapes. There are kits to make some of these, or you can devise your own shapes and sizes for a unique lampshade using the template information in Chapter 1. It is possible also to contact a frame maker for bespoke sizes of ring sets to create your own sizes (*see* Suppliers).

Straight Sided Hard Lampshades

For straight sided lampshades such as hexagonal and rectangular, there are two key tips that will greatly help making these shapes.

1. Create Crisp Edges

Having straight, neat edges or sides will ensure a great finished result for your lampshade. The key to achieving this is to use a scorer and a bone folder, which will semi-score and perfectly flatten the laminate without cutting through it, and will not damage the surface. It is important that the scores are perfectly vertical and meet at matching points along the panel, as only then will the laminate be accurately folded into the correct straight positions.

2. Seam Positions

The seam of a straight sided lampshade can be placed in a corner so that it is as unobtrusive as possible; if it is in the middle of the back of the lampshade, this is what the eye will be drawn to.

Making a Straight Sided Lampshade

This tutorial teaches how to make a 15cm hexagonal lampshade (using a kit). However, the method is the same for all straight sided hard lampshades, such as square or rectangular. It is important to mark the laminate panel with placement points of the frame edges before the lampshade is actually made. This is because the frames have rounded edge points, and so are slightly larger than the side-to-side measurement.

First, follow the steps 1–6 for making hard lampshades using a kit as outlined in the tutorial in the 'Making Drum Lampshades' section earlier in this chapter. Then follow the tutorial here.

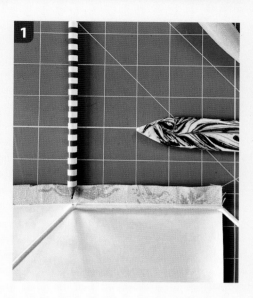

To mark out where the edges of the ring will go, place one edge of the frame at the start and along the top of the panel. It is useful having the double-sided tape, as it will stick in the exact place needed. Draw a mark at this edge point on the top of the panel, ensuring it is small – anything larger than 3mm will be seen after the shade has been made. Now 'roll' the frame to the next point and mark. Repeat this down the length of the panel.

The completed hexagonal lampshade: every side tells a story with this fabric design used in the tutorial for straight sided lampshades.

Remove the frame and, using a rule or grid, add marks along the base of the panel, exactly below those already drawn. It is important they line up exactly, so measure as you go. Place a ruler or grid, joining the first two marks. Then, using the scorer, score a line down, connecting the two points on the panel

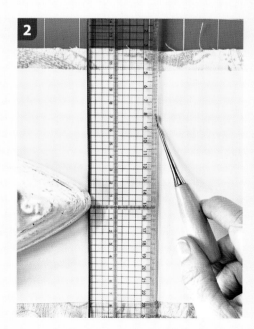

Once you have completed all the scoring, turn the panel over and fold over the panel at the first score lines; use the bone folder to press it down, creating a crisp edge but being careful with the fabric. Work along the length of the panel, folding over and pressing. There will be the smaller seam section at the end.

Continued on the following page.

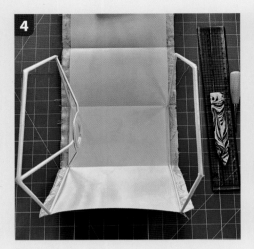

Renew the double-sided tape on the frame. Place the light-fitting end of the frame in the relevant position – that is, at the top or base of the panel, avoiding the gimbal, and the plain end of the frame on the opposite edge. Roll the frame along carefully, ensuring the corner edges meet the scored lines.

Snip away the fabric around the gimbals and tuck under the fabric under the rings using an old credit card. Leave the seam area until the end. At the corners there will be more bulk than with a drum, so make a very small snip at the edge, fold under slightly, and tuck under.

The Scallop Lampshade

A scallop lampshade is a lovely addition to the decor of any room and the scallops themselves add an attractive design detail, particularly for plain fabric lampshades. Scallop lampshades can be made having just one top ring, either with a duplex fitting, a clip-on bulb fitting, or with a drop-down fitting (*see* 'Ring Sets and Fittings' in Chapter 1). No base ring is used. However, it is worth using double-sided laminate to add strength to the shape.

An Important Note on Double-Sided Laminate

When you order double-sided laminate, it will arrive rolled up. Even after cutting the panel piece for the lampshade and weighing it down, it may have a tendency to return to its rolled up state. Because there is no base ring in these lampshades, ensure that the direction you form the lampshade is in the opposite direction to the original rolled direction of the laminate – this will stop it warping.

Making a Scalloped Hard Lampshade

In order to make the scalloped edge to the lampshade, start off by making a single scallop shape, cut out from a piece of card. You will then draw around this repeatedly along the base length of a lampshade laminate panel. However, it is useful to first create a complete card template that has all the scallops cut along the length because it can then be re-used to make further lampshades of this size. A scallop template like this (made from pink card) will form the basis of the tutorial.

First Steps

- After choosing the size of lampshade you wish to have, first either make or purchase a French drum lampshade template (*see* Chapter 1 for detail and how-to).
- The height of your scalloped lampshade must be chosen so that the lamp base fitting is hidden, and this means measuring to the top of the scallop and not the base edge. Bear this in mind when ordering a template.
- Order some double-sided laminate, draw around the lampshade template on this, and carefully cut out.
- Now decide the width and height of the scallops required, and work out how many at what size will fit equally around the base of the lampshade (being mindful of the seam allowance).

For this tutorial, the laminate template is for a lampshade with these dimensions: top diameter 15cm, base diameter 25cm, height 17.5cm. The scallop sizes have been calculated as follows:

- The circumference of the base of the finished lampshade is 78.5cm (25cm × pi (3.14) = 78.5cm).
- It will have 10 scallops, 2.5cm in height.
- Dividing 78.5cm by 10 results in each scallop being 7.85cm wide, but as the scallops are 2.5cm high, then this slightly reduces the finished base diameter of the lampshade (as we will be cutting into the height). The scallops should therefore be slightly smaller, and so 7.5cm works well. Note that any slight variations in individual scallops' size will not matter as they will be effectively undetectable.

It is a good idea to sketch the scallops in advance on the panel to ensure they will fit around the finished lampshade, and tweak a little if needed. On the template, allow 15mm for the seam, and draw that in advance too.

Fabrics and Papers for Scallop Shades
As well as using fabrics and papers for scalloped lamp-shades like those used in the tutorials so far, other good materials to use are hessian or raffia, which are easy to work with. Papers such as Japanese *washi* paper look amazing when lit, as does parchment, which has a slubby detail. All of these can be paired with a bias trim or left as they are. You can also simply use a strong card on its own, providing you ensure LED bulbs are used and it is treated with a flame retardant spray solution.

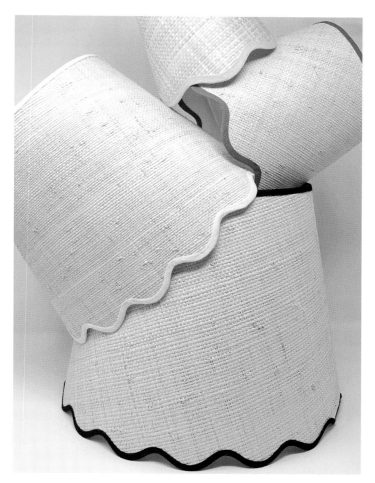

These scallop lampshades have been hand-crafted by Light Stylist, a team of lampshade makers based in England who specialise in natural materials and bespoke designs.

Sometimes simple is best – this scallop lampshade was made using plain card in a sunshine yellow, which sits on a beautiful lamp base, hand decorated by Cambridge House.

CREATING THE SCALLOP PATTERN

The scallop size is 7.5cm wide × 2.5cm high.

1. Measure and draw the width 7.5cm on a piece of card or stiff paper.
2. Then draw a mark at the halfway point (3.75cm). Measure and draw 2.5cm down from that point, using a rule or square to be accurate.
3. Draw a curve on one side, joining the end and base point, either by eye or use part of a circular item with the right sized curve, such as the base of a glass. This of course, can be drawn on a computer as well.
4. Then fold over down the middle line and cut out the shape, thus ensuring you have a symmetrical scallop shape.

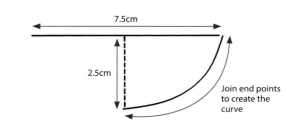

Scallop Template: make a template for the chosen-size scallops for your lampshade. For the tutorial, the width is 7.5cm and the height is 2.5cm.

TUTORIAL: MAKING A SCALLOPED HARD LAMPSHADE

Follow the tutorial to make a scalloped lampshade. This has a chalk-white linen lining, and pink linen on the outside, with bias trim. Background paper by Wanderlust.

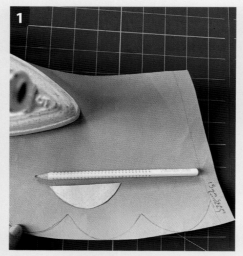

Place the French drum lampshade template on a table and the pink paper underneath it. Draw and cut around this so they are the same size. Mark the 15mm seam allowance at one end. Starting at the seam line, place the cut-out scallop pattern and draw around this. Continue along the length until you meet the end, checking they are all at the same angle and position. Cut out around the scallops, keeping the small extra piece at the seam area.

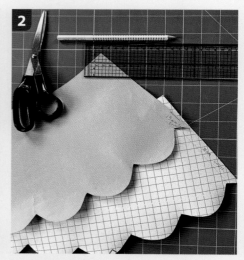

Place the completed scallop template onto the double-sided laminate (*see* note above on using this with the curve in the right direction) and draw all around it with pencil, placing weights on top for accuracy. It helps at this point to write 'top' on the laminate paper so there is no confusion about which side is which. Carefully cut all around the pattern, keeping the scallops neat and even.

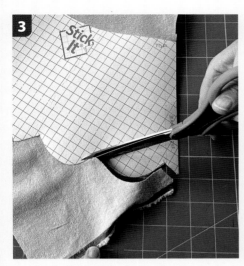

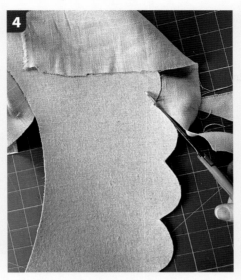

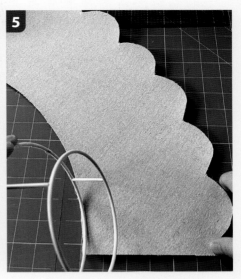

After ironing it well, attach the fabric of choice on the underside of the laminate panel (see 'Making Drum Lampshades' for technique in Chapter 2). This will be the lining of the lampshade, so choose a warm colour or one that harmonises with the outer cover. Trim all excess lining fabric carefully away once it has been adhered.

Now iron the fabric for the outer cover smooth and adhere this to the outside of the laminate panel. Draw a 6mm wide vertical line down the edge that will be the outer seam, and add a strip of double-sided tape to this for a neat seam. Remove the tape cover and fold the fabric over. Add another strip of double-sided tape on the opposite edge, on the outside, but keep the cover on the tape at this stage. Trim away the rest of the fabric to the edges.

Place 9mm of double-sided tape around the top ring; remove the cover. Position it on the end of the laminate without the folded-over fabric. Position it so that none of the gimbals are at the edge. Roll to the end, angling the ring in line with the panel. Add bulldog clips if needed. At the end, remove the cover of the tape at the seam and stick together, first ensuring the base line joins at the right position, that is, so the scallops adjoin properly.

To complete the lampshade, attach a bias binding trim to fit around the curves, both for decorative detail and to hide the cut edges. Add 18mm bias binding (see Chapter 8 on making trims) around the top ring (see 'Working with Paper' tutorial earlier in this chapter). Attach the bias around the scalloped base edge – it is fiddly but with a flexible-stretch bias binding you will have a good result. Cut a length for the base, plus 4cm extra for the scallops and seam.

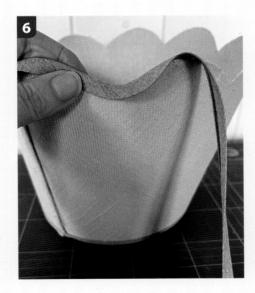

Beginning at the seam, leave the edges of the bias binding closed, and place one half of the bias binding on the underneath and one half around the front, the cut end being in line with the seam line.

Place either 6mm of double-sided tape or fabric glue to both sides of the bias to attach it to the front and back of the scallops around the base. Ensure it is placed right to the edge of the binding, otherwise it will gape open. Do a little at a time, and pull the binding right up into the scallop. Add bulldog clips while drying if using glue. Tuck the end into the folded-over other end to complete.

CHAPTER 3

FURTHER IDEAS AND TECHNIQUES FOR HARD LAMPSHADES

There are many more types of lampshades you can make using the hard materials, such as pleated paper or mini lampshade garlands. In addition, you can remake much-loved damaged or vintage hard lampshades, make huge oversized lampshades for large spaces, or have tiered lampshades – perfect for a high hallway. To make something truly bespoke, you can also design and print or block print your own fabric or paper, or hand paint your own designs.

DESIGNING YOUR OWN BESPOKE LAMPSHADES

The designers and artists featured here have produced truly original lighting with their own beautifully created range of lampshades using a variety of individual art practices.

Getting Your Own Designs Printed

There are fabric printers who print designs to order and this is ideal for individuals and small design studios. If you provide them with a digital file of the design, they will then print it on a range of fabrics, from fine cotton to heavier linen (swatches of the fabrics can be ordered in advance). Once submitted, you can purchase samples of your designs on their fabrics, to see the look and scale before you go ahead. Note that the fabrics will be white or natural in colour, therefore you may need to add a background colour into the design if required.

Lampshades designed and made by Alison Bick, who edits her illustrations digitally in order to get the designs printed onto linen and cotton fabrics.
(PHOTO: ANYA RICE)

ALISON BICK DESIGNS

Illustrator Alison Bick makes lampshades with fabric that has been printed with her designs. Alison draws floral- and coastal-inspired illustrations using vector-based software called Adobe Illustrator. This allows her to adapt her designs by scaling to any size or using bespoke colours chosen to suit her customers' decor. Each fabric lampshade template is printed digitally in the UK, and Alison makes her lampshades to order.

Alison Bick making her lampshades, all of which are created by having her designs printed to order on linen and cotton fabrics.
(PHOTO: LIZ KAY PHOTOGRAPHY)

Seascape Collection:
The place to be is by the sea

Marie creates her seascape lampshade designs from her original sketches and paintings, taking inspiration from the shorelines of the south coast of England. They are then digitally altered to achieve the right proportion to fit a lampshade-sized fabric panel. The panels are digitally printed and Marie then makes all her lampshades by hand in her studio for her lampshade art and design business, Parlour Made.

Marie's designs are created by first making sketches and paintings, which are then printed onto fabric for her lampshades. (PHOTO: JOHNNY GALLAGHER)

Hand-Decorated Lampshades

Using the methods outlined in Chapter 2, you can make hard lampshades using plain art paper attached to a laminate panel, or simply using paper or card with no backing (ensuring LED bulbs are used for fire retardancy). The advantage of having the laminate panel is that it will add depth to the lampshade design when lit. Decorate them either by hand painting or using cut stamps or blocks. These are particularly pleasing on empire and French drum lampshades as they can be decorated in relation to the shape – for example painting a check or gingham design means the stripes and checks can be perfectly positioned in relation to the lampshade shape itself.

The laminate panel can either be cut out, with the outer art paper attached in advance and hand decorated, or it can be decorated once the lampshade has been made. Adding bias binding complements the design of the lampshade. Paints to be used can be watercolour, acrylic, and gouache, as well as emulsion (use tester pots). Try different types on samples of the chosen paper or fabric covering to test for colour as well as depth and durability. Hold them in front of a light bulb to see the completed result in advance.

SOPHIA FRANCES STUDIO

Designer Sophia Frances commissioned a bespoke template for a small empire lampshade, drew around this on special art paper, and cut out the panels. Using watercolours, she then hand painted her exquisite designs across the art papers, each one having a different design. These were then adhered to laminate panels and made into lampshades suitable for table or desk lamps. In addition, each shade had a different colour bias binding trim attached, adding more colour to her beautiful artworks.

Designer Sophia Frances hand paints her beautiful designs in watercolour on special art paper for her lampshades.

Block Printing

Block printing and screen printing your own designs onto fabric or paper is another medium through which to create bespoke lighting designs and make truly individual lampshades.

For block printing, it is possible to purchase pre-carved blocks, or you can create and carve your own designs, which will allow you to plan where the blocks will be positioned, ensuring good pattern placement. For block printing onto fabric, use ink for fabrics. There are many online art shops that offer these, as well as the materials suitable for block printing. You can block print on natural fabrics, such as cotton, linen, and rayon, and some synthetic fabrics (but test a piece first), as well as on good papers.

ANNA VOJTISEK

Pattern and textile designer Anna Vojtisek produces a beautiful collection of lampshades using traditional block-printing techniques. She first carves out the blocks with her designs and then, using eco-friendly water-based inks, repeat-prints onto fabric and paper. Some of her designs are also litho printed using vibrant vegetable-based inks on FSC-certified matt paper. She then makes the lampshades in a variety of shapes and sizes, and as each is made to order, there is limited wastage of resources.

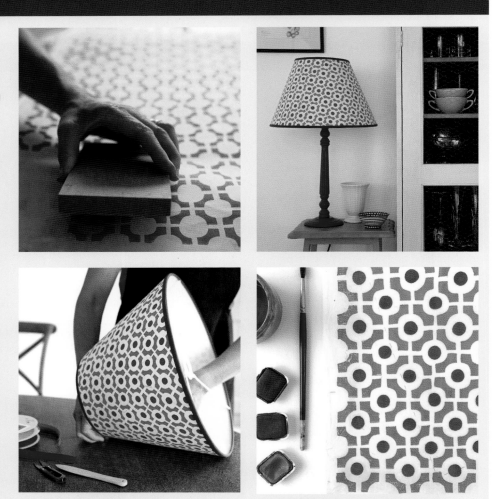

Anna Vojtisek making her lampshade with her block print design Milano lampshade, Raspberry.

Screen Printing

Screen printing your own fabric is another idea for producing lovely individual designs. There are kits available online as well as workshops to learn the techniques. Screen printing is a process where the ink is pushed through a mesh screen onto fabric or paper around a stencilled design – the stencil stops the ink going onto that part of the fabric and hence the design is revealed.

JANE ELLISON TEXTILES

Textile designer Jane Ellison screen prints her own colourful designs onto natural fabrics using a hand silk-screen process. Fabrics are made into varying custom-sized lampshades. Her bold, graphic patterns are inspired by mid-twentieth-century artists and architecture. The shapes are drawn and cut into paper stencils or processed photographically onto screens. She then prints the fabric using eco-conscious water-based inks in batches, repeating the design onto each piece of fabric. Finished fabrics are attached to heavy paper board and rolled into shape. Paper is preferred for sustainability and to give a softer, diffused light.

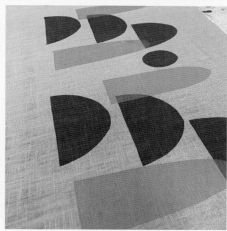

From a screen print on fabric to finished lampshades. Jane Ellison's 'Conil' Lampshade in Caramel, Peach & Brown.

Cyanotype Printing

Cyanotype printing is one of the oldest photographic printing practices in photography. The characteristic feature is its shade of blue – cyan – which results from the chemicals used and their exposure to ultraviolet light from the sun.

BRIDGET ARNOLD

Bridget Arnold collects plants locally then uses cyanotype printing to capture them. Two chemicals that become sun sensitive when mixed together are then painted onto 100 per cent cotton fabric. The plants are laid on the fabric, and glass is then placed on top and exposed to ultraviolet light. They are left to develop until the colour has altered, taken off the frame, and rinsed several times to wash the chemicals out to fix them. When it is dry, the fabric is ready to use to make wonderful bespoke lampshades.

Bridget forages plants locally then uses cyanotype printing to capture them to make her wonderful lampshades.

OVERSIZED LAMPSHADES

Although lampshades over 40cm diameter do not seem particularly large, especially for large room ceiling lights or standard lamps, there can be an issue in the size of the fabric width or paper width being used to make them. The standard width of soft furnishing fabrics is around 137cm; therefore this will only fit around a drum panel used for a 40cm lampshade. If your fabric is plain, it can be railroaded (that is, turned 90 degrees, or the height used as the width), in which case a longer length can be cut to make large lampshades. If the fabric has a vertical stripe, and is railroaded, it will have stripes going horizontally, which may work well; of course, if using a check fabric then the pattern is the same in both directions and it can be railroaded without problems. It is worth bearing in mind that railroaded fabric will be more expensive, as the meterage is sold by the vertical height.

However, most lampshades are made using fabrics that have a horizontal fixed pattern, or a graphic that needs to run widthways. If the lampshade is being made to match other items in the room, such as curtains and blinds, then you will definitely want the pattern to run as it is meant to. In this case, widths of this fabric will need to be joined so that it will fit around the circumference of the larger lampshade rings.

Making an Oversized Lampshade

Refer to the table in Chapter 1 that gives the length of fabric needed for the various-sized lampshades. Remember to factor in more for your large lampshade as there will need to be a new seam and the pattern may need to be matched. You can have joined fabric or paper with the seams close to each other, but this really only works for a lampshade that will be positioned where the back of it is not visible, for example on a corner desk. For ceiling lampshades, however, it is advisable to position a new seam exactly opposite the main seam, for symmetry. One long piece of the laminate can be cut to size, but two pieces of fabric or paper will be needed to make the larger lampshade.

Large lampshades can be made using fabric or paper lengths by creating a new seam placed opposite the main seam for symmetry.

For accuracy, it is easier to make these lampshades in a different way from the normal method. This time, the laminate panel will be first placed on the table, paper side up, and the joined fabric or paper on top, face up (pattern side up). This will ensure the new seam will be positioned directly opposite the main seam. As recommended by the manufacturers, please note it is a good idea to use the extra-rigid laminate to make larger lampshades (over 40cm), as it is more robust for holding the weight of the fabric.

The following specifications are used in the tutorial:

- The lampshade is a drum with a 45cm diameter.
- The length of panel = 142cm, plus a 1.5cm seam allowance = 143.5cm.

- The halfway point, less the 1.5cm seam allowance, is 71cm from one end. This is where the new seam will be positioned.
- Fabric length: 145cm plus 1cm folded-over neat edge and another 1cm for the pattern match join = 147cm minimum. We will join two lengths and pattern match.
- The fabric being used in the tutorial has a width of 130cm, therefore two (pattern matched) pieces of 73.5cm each will be used. You can use longer lengths, pattern match and then cut to size if preferred.

The tutorial uses individual components. However, kits are available for large size lampshades too.

TUTORIAL: MAKING AN OVERSIZED LAMPSHADE

The completed oversized lampshade, using two pieces of fabric that are perfectly pattern matched.

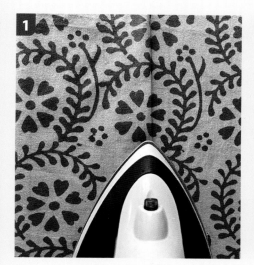

In order for the fabric to be the right length, first join the two fabric pieces. Lay the two fabric lengths on the table and decide where the new seam will be on the pattern. Turn under 1cm of one edge of the fabric, fold it under, and, ensuring the pattern matches, iron the two pieces together.

Add double-sided tape (9mm) to this 1cm fold, take off the cover, and adhere it to the right-hand piece of fabric. Once you have joined the two fabrics together using the sticky tape so they perfectly pattern match, trim away any excess of the right-hand fabric underneath to 1cm. The fabric is now one longer length.

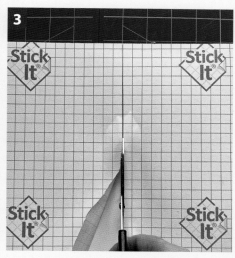

To find the middle point of the laminate panel, measure from one end to the halfway point (71cm) and put pencil marks both top and base at this point. Draw a vertical line connecting them. Slide a pin in the base at the pencil mark to open it up, and then cut the paper up the line. Lightly mark the middle points on the sticky part of the panel, top and base.

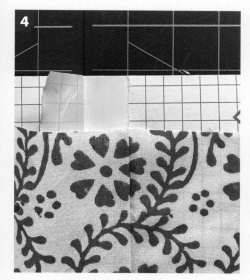

Peel away a little of the laminate cover paper on the left-hand side; position the ironed fabric on top, with the fabric's new seam perfectly in line with the right-hand vertical edge of the paper in place. Remember to leave 15mm extra top and base horizontal edges for tucking in (*see* tutorial on making drum lampshades not using a kit).

Peel more of the laminate's paper cover away a little at a time on the left; using an old credit or store card to smooth down the fabric and avoid any creases, work down the whole length on the left side. Then repeat the process on the right-hand side to attach the fabric. Once completed, make the lampshade as outlined in the 'Using Separate Components to Make a Drum Lampshade' tutorial (Chapter 2).

Not Enough Fabric or Paper to Fit around the Lampshade

If you are using paper, it may be so narrow that the maximum length of laminate it will fit will be to make a 15cm drum lampshade. Use the previous tutorial to work with paper, patten matching, and positioning the new seam opposite the main one.

If for any reason you do not have enough fabric to pattern match for a new seam, but you are using a paper or fabric with a random or really small pattern, the new seam may work as it will merge in with the rest of the design. However, for larger patterns, it will look messy and the eye will be drawn to it. A solution is to place a matching or contrasting bias trim vertically down the join, which again is positioned opposite the main seam. In addition, you can add some over the main seam – it can even look like an intentional design feature! This is particularly effective if the trim matches the colour of the inside of the lampshade.

Because gift-wrap paper is narrow, widths can be pattern matched and joined to make varying sized lampshades.
(PHOTO: CAITLIN WARREN)

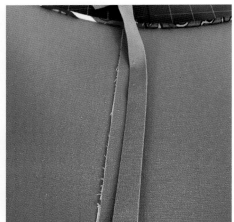

If there is not enough fabric to make your chosen size of lampshade and pattern match, use bias binding in a harmonising colour and place it over the main seam, as well as the new joined seam opposite. Here, it matches the inside of the lampshade too.

TIERED PENDANT LAMPSHADES

There are lampshade-making kits to create tiered hard lampshades, where you have a larger top drum and smaller drums hanging below it, with either two, three, or four lampshades in a tier. You can have fun with these using complementary fabric colours, and even run one large design down the total length of the lampshades. They are perfect for being hung at the top of stairwells and in high-ceilinged rooms.

A kit for a two-tier lampshade, for example, has four rings. Two are for the larger top lampshade, one being a utility ring and the other a ring with hooks fitted around it. This first larger lampshade is made using the drum lampshade method in Chapter 2. Ensure the utility ring is positioned in the top of the lampshade, and the ring with the hooks at the base. The smaller lampshade is then made using two plain rings. When complete, the smaller lampshade is placed just inside the larger one and attached onto its ring using the hooks. Make sure the seams of the two lampshades are lined up. You can also place a diffuser inside the smaller lampshade base.

ACCORDION PLEATED LAMPSHADES – PAPER AND FABRIC

Accordion pleated lampshades are made with paper- or fabric-covered laminate folded neatly into a series of equal-sized pleats in alternating directions. They can be made using lovely papers, wallpapers, or fabrics.

Making Accordion Pleated Lampshades

These lampshades have a small top diameter compared to the wide base diameter, and have regular accordion pleats – usually between 1–2.5cm in size, although you can make them to your own-sized design. They are made using fabric or paper adhered to a thin, less-rigid laminate backing, and then accordion pleated along this panel. The inside of the pleats are then hole punched and, when cut, clipped neatly onto the top ring of a lampshade frame.

They can also be made using paper or card without the laminate backing, in which case it is best to use a good weight of paper to give body to the pleats. The two ends of the panel are joined together by machine sewing down

'Flamingo Dream' lampshade made by Charlotte Tot Jensen at Lampshades DK. Charlotte used three tiers to showcase the large vertical design on the fabric. Tiered lampshades are perfect for hallways or high-ceilinged rooms.

The accordion pleated lampshade – these are currently enjoying a resurgence in popularity. Paper by Molly Mahon.

the seam, although due to the small-sized widths of some papers, two panels may be needed, with the extra seam being positioned opposite the main seam. If you are using plain fabric or paper, it can be railroaded, thereby only needing one seam. The most important thing to get right when making these lampshades is that each pleat/fold is precisely the same size, and that the punched holes line up exactly with each other.

How Many Pleats?

You can choose how many pleats to have, although there must be enough to fit comfortably around the base ring of the frame. The more pleats there are, the greater difference there will be between the top and base measurements, as the cover will flare out more from the top. If the pattern on your paper or fabric is one you wish to see more of, use fewer and wider pleats, meaning the pattern will be more visible.

A GUIDE TO THE LENGTH OF MATERIALS NEEDED FOR ACCORDION LAMPSHADES

Finished pleat size	Size needed for pleat	Number of pleats	Length of material
1.5cm	3cm	× 30	= 90cm (plus 2.5mm each end for the join*)
1.5cm	3cm	× 36	= 108cm (ditto)
2cm	4cm	× 30	= 120cm (ditto)
2cm	4cm	× 36	= 144cm (ditto)

Notes: The height of the panel should be the measurement of the slope height of the lampshade frame, plus a minimum of 2cm for the top and 2.5cm at the base. For the tutorial example, this will be 19.5cm. Consider the lamp base you will be using – note that if it is flaring out more, you may need more height to the lampshade as the frame may be visible at the base.

* The width needs 2.5mm at each end to machine sew the seam. However, if using a narrow paper, then two sections will be needed for the length, requiring 2.5mm at each end of the pieces.

Getting Started

The sizing instructions for the tutorial are as follows:

- The frame has a top-ring diameter of 8cm, base ring diameter of 23cm, and slope height of 15cm. The frame has three struts and a candle-bulb fitting. (This size works well for smaller and medium-sized lampshades; however, you can get different sized frames made to order for your own size choices, or find vintage ones to re-use.)
- There will be thirty-six pleats (2cm wide each), and therefore twelve folds will fit between each of the three struts.
- The completed lampshade will have the following measurements once on the frame: top diameter 8cm, base diameter 32cm, height 19.5cm. However, if you place your cover on a larger frame (providing it fits around the base circumference), you will have a larger lampshade.
- As the pleats are 2cm wide, 4cm is needed to create each one. Multiplying this by thirty-six means that 144cm of both the laminate and the outer decorative paper is needed, plus a seam.
- Because 144cm is wider than the printed paper, there will be two pieces of 72cm each, plus 2.5mm for each end (this is the seam allowance to machine sew them together), so each section will be 72.5cm.
- Therefore, cut out two laminate panels, each one sized at 72.5cm (width/length) × 19.5cm (height).
- Cut two pieces of your chosen decorative paper or (ironed) fabric slightly larger than the panel size, ensuring your pattern matches across both pieces if applicable.

You will need the following for this tutorial:

- lampshade frame – with a narrow top ring and much wider base ring
- your chosen fabric or paper
- length of laminate material, using the lighter weight one available, if using
- pencil
- ruler
- bone folder
- scorer – the one shown in the photo is a wooden-handled awl
- hole puncher
- rubber/eraser
- scissors
- sewing machine
- thread colour matched to your laminate or inside of your paper

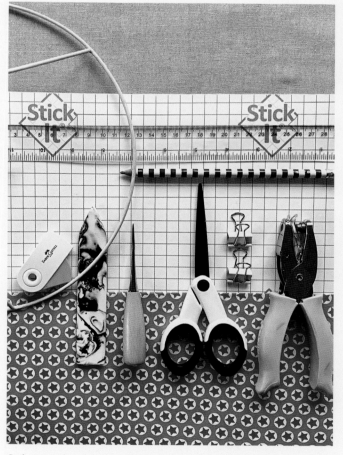

Gather together the materials needed to make the accordion lampshade.

1

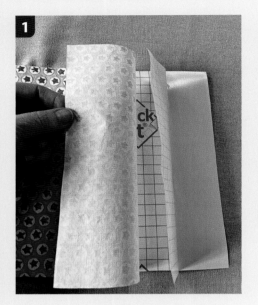

Place the decorative paper or (ironed) fabric face up over the laminate panel. Peel back a small section of the laminate's paper cover and smooth down the paper/fabric onto it. Release the laminate paper a little at a time, smoothing your paper or fabric onto it to the end. Trim away any excess fabric or paper all around the panel. Repeat for the second piece.

2

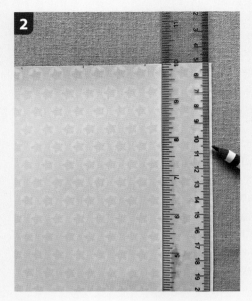

Turn the laminate panel face up and make very small pencil marks 2.5mm in from one vertical end, both top and base, and join these marks using a ruler and pencil. This is the seam line to machine sew down later on. Then place small pencil dots every 4cm in from that drawn line along the horizontal top and base lengths, ensuring accuracy.

3a

3b

4

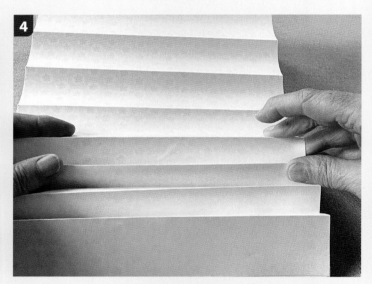

Place your ruler from one pencil dot at the top to the one vertically below it and, using an awl, score a line connecting them. Repeat this along the length at every 4cm mark. There will be the 2.5mm at the end for the seam allowance. Now fold the first scored line upwards, making it as crisp as you can. Work along the length. (Usually, in accordion pleating, the scored line would be folded downwards however we do not want to damage the paper/fabric of the lampshade.)

With laminate side up, take the edge of the first 4cm fold and push it over to meet the second 4cm fold line, pinching the scored lines together to make a downwards fold at the midway point, that is, at 2cm. Ensure they are lined up. Use the bone folder to score the new fold underneath. It is important that all the folds are the same size, so check before you make the scores. Work along the whole panel and, when finished, fold up the first and last 2cm pleats.

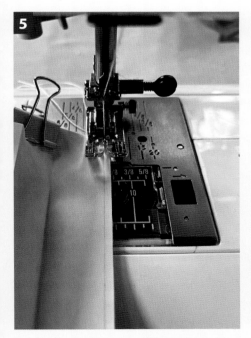

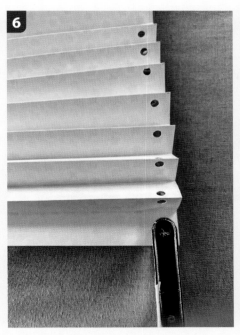

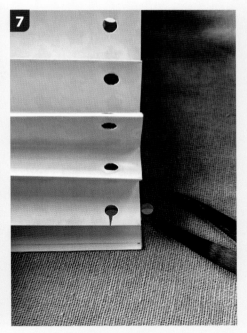

Repeat for the second piece of fabric/paper and now join them together: lay the joined edges on the sewing machine and machine sew down the pencil mark, which will be 2.5mm from the edge (it helps to slightly flatten them first and use a clip to hold them in place). Use a normal-sized stitch and tension, with the same colour thread as the fabric or paper on the panel. You now have one long length panel.

Place a light pencil mark at the point that is 2cm down from the top edge and halfway into each scored inner fold. Repeat for each fold along the panel. It is important they are as accurately placed as possible in the same position. Then, using your hole punch, make a hole with the pencil mark in the middle. Work along the panel, but do not punch the very last hole – this will be done after sewing the seam to ensure it lines up.

Scissor snip into each punched hole, at the fold edge on the inside of the panel, as shown. There needs to be two snips starting at the same place but one going slightly to the left and one slightly to the right at the hole. Then, still laminate side up, machine sew down the last seam 2.5mm in. Make snips at the last punched hole at the machined seam (do not worry, it will not come apart). Make your last hole punch, ensuring it lines up with its neighbouring one. Rub out all pencil marks.

Turn your lampshade cover inside out by stretching it open a little, putting your hands inside, holding the top and base edges, and turning it inside out. Attach it to your frame by pushing the cut holes onto the top ring. Ensure you share out the number of folds all the way around so it looks uniform, in this case twelve between each of the three struts.

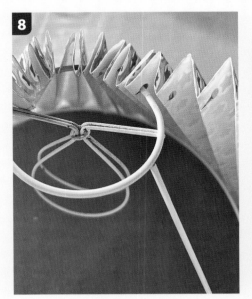

After attaching the cover, use your fingers to sharpen and crease the pleats and folds a final time, being careful of the paper or fabric used.

Decorative Detail for Accordion Pleated Lampshades

Adding Ribbon

It is possible to add thin ribbon or cord to the lampshade, both as a decorative detail and to pull the pleats closer together. Using your awl or a small hole punch, make small holes 2cm down and half way in from the punched holes that attach the lampshade to the frame. Use a large needle or a bodkin to thread your ribbon through the holes, ensuring you leave a length of approximately 10cm free at the start and the end on the outside of the lampshade. When on the lamp base, gently pull the ribbon and make a bow to tie the ends.

Attaching a ribbon can add a lovely decorative detail, as well as enabling you to pull the pleats closer together.

Use a bodkin or very large needle to thread a narrow ribbon through small punched holes, and tie a bow when you reach the end.

Frame Colours

As the lampshade is not lined, you can spray paint the frame or wrap ribbon around the top ring in a matching colour to your fabric or paper choice. This stops the white of the frame being visible. If spray painting, place the frame in a box outside on a good weather day, and spray two coats.

ACCORDION PLEATED LAMPSHADE MAKING TIPS

- If making a lampshade using paper or card only (that is, with no laminate), add another 2cm to the top and base heights, and fold these over before pleating and scoring. This will add strength to the area that you will hole punch at the top, and to the folds at the base, ensuring they are crisper.
- Spray the inside with a fire-retardant spray and use an LED bulb, as you are not using a fire-retardant material.
- Use a lampshade frame with three struts, especially if using paper only, as there is less metal to be seen.
- If all the pleats are exactly the same size and the holes punched at exactly the same place, your lampshade will be very successful!

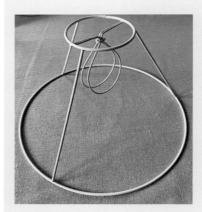

The best frames to use for accordion pleated lampshades are those with a small diameter top ring and larger-in-proportion base ring, and three struts. This is less fiddly to attach the pleated cover to than having the usual six struts. However, any cone shape with a very small top ring and wide base ring will work.

Take time to ensure that the pleats are all the same size and have been hole punched in the same position in every fold, so that a uniform look is achieved all the way around the lampshade.

LIBERTY FABRIC FAIRY LIGHT GARLAND

These lovely mini lampshades can be made using papers or fabric; however, the Liberty prints with their exquisite small print designs look particularly pleasing when lit up. Hang them around bedheads, shelving, and mantelpieces – they will brighten any space. They are lovely to make with friends or children, and are not expensive if using scraps of fabric and trim offcuts. The fabric is adhered to a paper cup using decoupage glue, which works particularly well because it dries quickly, clear, and smooth, and does not leave brush marks. Please note that as the light string has LED bulbs, the paper will not get too hot and they are therefore safe. However, it is best not to leave them unattended.

These little Liberty fabric lampshade garlands can be made using small scraps of fabric and trims, and placed all around the house.

TOOLS AND MATERIALS

You will need the following to make your little light garland:

- paper cups – 7oz size
- template
- pencil
- scissors
- LED fairy light string (in the tutorial there are ten, but they come in a variety of lengths to choose from)
- two AA batteries
- Liberty scraps of fabric, minimum size 23cm wide × 12cm high
- decoupage glue
- small paint brush
- thin 3mm double-sided tape
- a selection of trims

See Suppliers details for these materials.

Collect the materials needed in advance to make the little Liberty fabric lampshade garlands, plus use a plastic sheet or bag for the glue stage to protect your table.

First unroll the curled-up rim at the base of the paper cup and cut this away. Then, using one scissor end, make a small hole in the middle of the base of the cup. This base will actually be the top of the mini lampshade and have the light bulb pushed through it. Repeat for all the paper cups.

To make the template needed, wrap one of the cups with a piece of paper; then, using a pencil, draw around the curves of the top and base onto the paper. Alternatively, use baking parchment and draw lines on this, tracing the top and base edges of the cup. Cut template out and then transfer it onto a piece of stiff card.

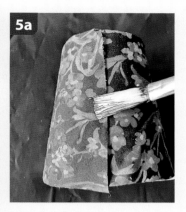

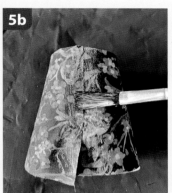

Iron your selected fabrics. They need to be approximately 23cm wide × 12cm high. Now place one face down and put the template on top – take note of the pattern. Trace around this with a pencil/chalk and cut out using sharp scissors. Repeat for all ten lampshades.

Place a plastic cover on your table at this stage to protect it from the glue. Using the brush, smooth a layer of the decoupage glue all over one cup, holding the edges to keep your fingers glue-free. Then add the fabric strip, starting at the seam of the cup; gently pull (as it can wrinkle) and smooth the fabric down as you go around.

Now add strips of double-sided tape around the top and base of each cup, take off the cover, and add the trim. There are many trims to choose from – ricrac, tassels, pompoms, velvet ribbon, glitter ribbon, and so on – but ensure the one you use is narrow so it is in proportion. Start at the seam, attach, and at the end cut the trim so it just meets the first piece; the tape will stop it from fraying.

Once all the trims have been added to the cups, work out which order you would like them to be in and line them up. Now push in the top of the first LED bulb into the hole in the base of the cup – holding it at an angle helps. Add all the others along the string of lights. Add batteries to the box and switch on!

At the end, add more glue under the fabric seam/overlap, smooth it down, and glue lightly over the seam – it will look a little white and messy but it will dry clear. Move immediately onto the next cup. Note that it is important to do one cup at a time, as the glue dries very quickly. When you have finished all ten, cut away all excess fabric around the cup edges.

THE QUICK-MAKE GATHERED LAMPSHADE

It is possible to use a hard lampshade as the foundation for a quick-make gathered fabric lampshade, and although it is not the traditional method of making gathered or pleated lampshades (*see* Chapter 6), it can still give a pleasing result.

Getting Started

Either hand make or purchase a hard lampshade in the size of your choice – one with an outer cover in a neutral colourway is ideal, as it will not fight with the outer cover fabric design and acts as a lining. For this tutorial the hard lampshade has the following dimensions:

- top ring 13.5cm
- base ring 20cm
- slope height 16cm.

Refer to the 'Gathering Fabric Methods' tutorial in Chapter 4, which teaches you how to gather fabric quickly using a sewing machine, or by hand using running stitch. In this example, the base ring fabric has been gathered on a sewing machine, and the top ring fabric hand sewn to make the gathers.

The completed quick-make gathered lampshade, created by gathering and attaching fabric to a hard lampshade. Fabric supplied by Haines.

TOOLS AND MATERIALS

For the quick-make gathered lampshade, the following materials are required:

- handmade or shop-bought hard lampshade
- fabric for outer cover – thin or fine is best
- sewing machine, or needle and thread as alternative
- matching thread of colour of fabric or bias binding
- small bulldog clips, max width 2cm
- pencil
- grid rule or ruler
- strong textile glue
- ready-cut bias binding length or handmade bias binding (*see* Chapter 8).

It will already be fire retardant because you have the hard lampshade laminate material as the lining.

For the quick-make gathered lampshade, materials needed include a ready-made hard lampshade, glue, and bias binding.

Calculating How Much Fabric to Use

The amount of fabric needed for gathered lampshades is always based on the measurement of the base ring, and is then multiplied by the fullness you wish to have. Use thinner fabrics for making gathered lampshades, otherwise it will bunch up – *see* Chapter 6 for detail about which fabrics to use and the quantities needed for the frame sizes. For this tutorial:

- The circumference of the base ring is 20cm (diameter) × pi (3.14) = 63cm (rounded up).
- The fabric will have × 2 fullness = 126cm (63cm × 2), plus add 1cm each end for turning under = 128cm cut width.
- The height is calculated by measuring the height of the lampshade (16cm) then adding 3cm each to the top and base for a handling allowance = 22cm cut height.

TUTORIAL: A QUICK-MAKE GATHERED LAMPSHADE

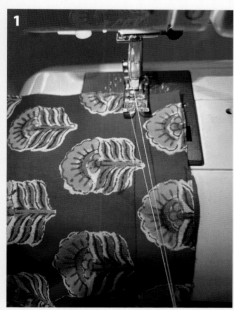

Iron the fabric and draw horizontal lines along the width – 3cm up from the base of the fabric and 3cm down from the top. Divide the fabric into four equal amounts – in this case 31.5cm – and mark on the fabric. Also mark four points on the top and base of the lampshade, that is, every quarter – the first one being at the seam. Gather the fabric using the gathering methods outlined in Chapter 4, either by using the sewing machine or using running stitch by hand.

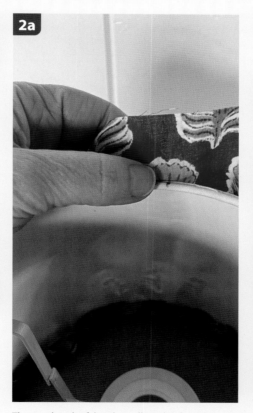

Then gather the fabric by pulling the threads, ensuring the gathers are shared equally around the length. Turn under 1cm at one end of the fabric (so there is no raw edge), and use a bulldog clip to attach it to the base of the frame, starting at the seam of the lampshade. Add clips where the pencil marks on the fabric meet the pencil marks on the lampshade. This ensures it is shared out equally. Turn the end under the last 1cm.

Continued on the following page.

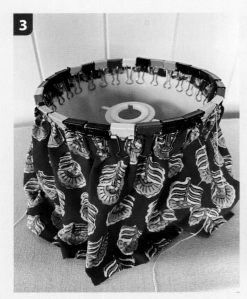

3

4a

4b

With the lampshade still with the base up, remove a few of the clips and place some glue on the underside of the fabric; adhere only on the front of the lampshade ring, not on the top. Now push this glued section of fabric onto the front of the ring, and reattach the bulldog clips – close together this time so all the fabric is held into place while it dries. Work all around the base ring. Once dry, take the clips off.

Now pull the fabric gathers up to the top ring so they are taut. In this tutorial, the base of the fabric is machined to gather it and running stitch is used for the top. After stitching, pull the needle to gather the fabric. Match the pencil marks on the fabric to meet the pencil marks on the lampshade frame. Repeat the glue method around the top, placing bulldog clips to hold it in place to dry.

5

6

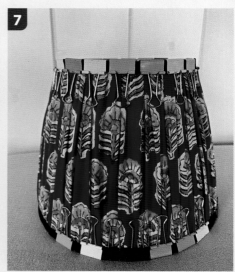

7

Once completely dry and secure, trim away the excess fabric around the rings so that it is neat. If necessary, add a smear of Fray Stop or a waxy glue to stop any fraying of the fabric and let it dry. Then either buy or make bias binding to complete the lampshade. The lampshade in this tutorial uses 18mm bought bias binding.

Place a strip of double-sided tape (9mm size) around the base and top front edges of the lampshade. Take the cover off and adhere one closed side of the bias binding to it. Now open up the other side of the bias and pull it up and over the ring. Push it underneath the ring (see 'Making a Lampshade Using Paper with a Bias Trim' in Chapter 2).

Alternatively, use textile glue if preferred, attaching the bias binding around the front of the top and base of the lampshade. Wait for it to dry and then pull over the bias and tuck under (again as outlined in Chapter 2). Attach bulldog clips all the way around until the glue is dry.

TRADITIONAL FRAMED HARD LAMPSHADES

These 'traditional-look' lampshades are made by attaching fabric-covered hard laminate materials onto a traditional full lampshade frame.

Making the Lampshade

Fabric is attached onto panels of laminate, and therefore a full design can be used across the lampshade; or you can mix and match different panels for interest. This lampshade-making method can be used on any full frame design or shape. However, note that there is no lining and therefore the metal struts will be visible on a ceiling lampshade – although if they are white they will fade into the white laminate used as the backing.

Using a full lampshade frame (*see* frame shapes in Chapter 4), you will need the following materials:

- choices of fabric – mix and match the panels or keep all the same
- binding or trim of choice
- scissors
- glue or strong double-sided tape
- laminate to cut to size
- cardboard to make a template
- pencil or pen.

Materials needed to make a panelled hard lampshade include a cardboard panel template of the area between any two struts.

This panelled vintage-style lampshade has been expertly handmade by Rachael Powell from Ooh La La Lampshades.

The completed lampshade, with added trims adhered with textile glue to the struts where the individual panels meet, and around the top and base rings.

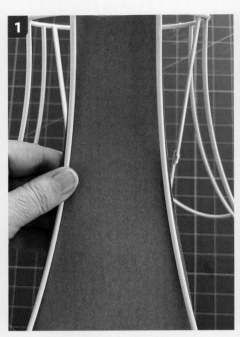

First make a template using some stiff card for the area between two struts, from the middle of each wire to the next.

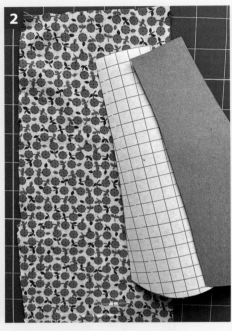

Draw round this template onto some laminate (the clear version is used here) and cut out.

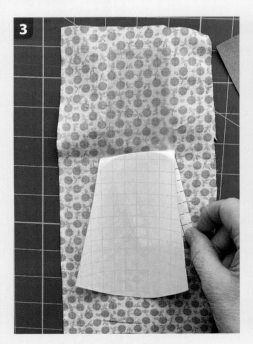

Attach ironed fabric onto the laminate by removing the backing paper and smoothing it down onto the back of the fabric.

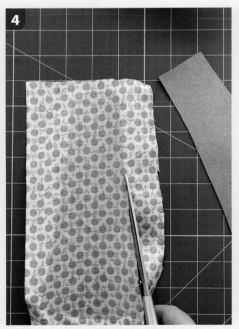

Trim away any excess fabric all around the laminate panel, including frays around the edges.

Repeat this so you have one for each section of the lampshade frame, using either the same fabric or a selection.

REMAKING HARD LAMPSHADES

There are three key reasons for remaking hard lampshades:

- Recycling, reusing and repurposing is always good.
- It is cost effective – you only need a length of the laminate, not new rings or a template.
- It is useful when the lampshade perfectly fits a particular lamp base.

Choose a fabric or paper where the pattern placement works well, especially for empire or cone shades, as you are confined to the original size of the lampshade.

Getting Started

In order to remake a hard lampshade, it is necessary to take apart the original as it is. Great care should be taken to do this, as often the old materials are liable to crack. The rings will then be reconditioned to use with new materials.

Follow the step-by-step instructions to breathe new life in to your lampshade, which will be ready to be used with its accompanying base. The effort to remake it is more rewarding, eco-friendly, and cost effective than buying a new one.

Now attach each panel to the frame either using strong glue or double-sided tape. Ensure they abut each other down the struts with no overlaps or gaps.

Now repeat around the frame. Then add a trim using textile glue along the struts, and around the top and base rings to hide all the raw edges.

Remaking lampshades is beneficial in many ways. This lampshade will be changed from being tired and tatty and will lose its dated appearance.

The lampshade has been given a new lease of life with new fabric and laminate. It is always good to recycle – it is cost effective and results in the lampshade sitting perfectly on its original lamp base.

TOOLS AND MATERIALS

You will have the lampshade rings already, and so the other items needed are:

- lampshade making basic kit as outlined in Chapter 1: double-sided tape, scissors, pencil, ruler, an old store card or knife
- length of laminate
- choice of fabric or paper to have on the outside of the lampshade
- file for rubbing down the old rings and/or white spirit to remove glue
- spray paint in white – PlastiKote is perfect for repurposing
- cardboard box
- knife for removing the current laminate panel.

As well as key lampshade-making materials, for remakes you will also need a file and/or white spirit, spray paint, and a sharp knife.

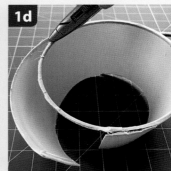

Using a sharp knife, and holding it facing away from you, carefully and accurately slice down the seam of the lampshade; cut between the rings and the laminate edge to remove the original lampshade panel. Carefully peel away the covered laminate – it is important this is left intact as it will form the template or pattern needed to make the new panel for the lampshade.

Lay the original panel, old cover side up, on top of a new piece of laminate, paper side up; draw around this. Add on 15mm at one end for the seam allowance. Attach the new fabric to the laminate, following the tuition in Chapter 2, allowing for the 15mm top and base horizontal edges (to tuck under the rings); place a 1cm fold over the seam edge, plus tabs.

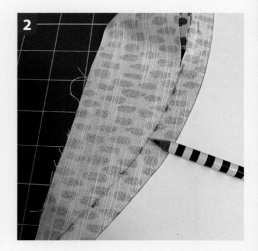

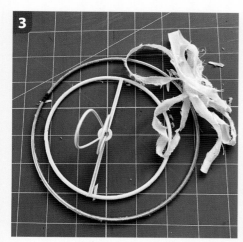

3

Now remove all the old glue, fabric, or damaged paint from the rings. It helps to use a file or sandpaper to remove hard paint, and white spirit for dried old glue. Even putting the rings in a dishwasher can help! Once smooth, and to prevent rust coming through in the future, respray the rings with PlastiKote primer and paint.

4a

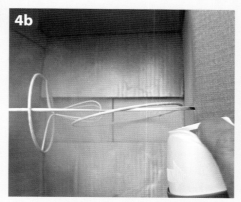

4b

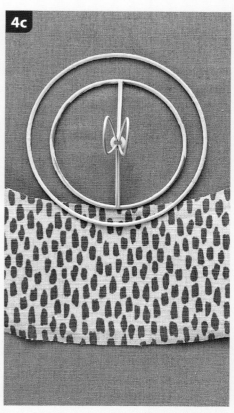

4c

Place the rings in a box and spray, leave to dry, and then repeat, moving the rings each time so that they are all covered. Use primer first if your rings are bare metal, then the white spray paint. It helps to put a rod through the box to keep the rings from being in contact with the box.

Once the rings are ready, make the lampshade as per the instructions in Chapter 2. Adding a trim will further enhance the appearance of the original, very plain and in bad condition lampshade. This lampshade is now revived and refreshed, and will still fit the original lamp base it was supplied with.

5

TROUBLESHOOTING HARD LAMPSHADE MAKING

When making hard lampshades, you may come across problems and challenges. Use these troubleshooting tips to help out.

TROUBLESHOOTING HARD LAMPSHADE MAKING

Issue	Cause	Solution
The seam has come unstuck	Fabric challenge	Use a smear of super glue or stronger double-sided tape
The seam will not stick at all	Using wool or velvet	Sew slip stitch down the outside of the seam (*see* 'Keeping the Seams Closed' section)
The seam inside is gaping	Tape only on outside edge of seam	Add two pieces of tape to the seam. Also cover the inside with bias tape or other (*see* 'Keeping the Seams Closed' section)
Fabric is visible on the inside at the seam area	Seam too narrow	Cut away some of the fabric, leaving a gap in the seam
Fabric is popping away	Usually silk or treated fabric or calico can pop in hot conditions	Try a sample with these first; smooth away with credit card, hoping they will stay flat
The fabric is too short to go under the rings	Fraying fabric or using a thick fabric	Cut more fabric along horizontal edges
There is not enough fabric at the seam to be tucked under the rings	Using thicker fabric	Add tabs of extra fabric
Fabric puckers over the rings	Fabric too thin	Add soft cotton wool on top of the rings before tucking
The pattern is 'off' along the top of the lampshade	The panel is not placed along horizontal pattern repeat	Place pins along the length, matching the pattern detail
The utility ring fitting is sticking out of the lampshade	It has been put in upside down	Ease it out of the shade and replace, and then tuck in
The fitting is too low down for the lamp base	Every lamp base is different and fittings can show	Use a duplex fitting with a shade carrier for your lampshade
The seam is bowing inwards	The seam has been closed too early	Leave the sticking of seams and tucking of fabric under the rings in the seam area until the end of making the lampshade
There are threads showing at snips by gimbals	Cut fabric	Add Fray Stop onto fabric before snipping into it
There is a dark vertical mark on the kit laminate	It has been rolled up and the end has stuck, picking up dust	Use a baby wipe, a rubber, or white spirit to remove
The lampshade has hard edges around the rings	The rings were positioned a little too far on the panel	Either remake or learn to love it!

Keeping the Seams Closed

Perhaps the most common issues with hard lampshades are around the seam area. The seam may come apart over time, or even while being made if the fabric does not respond to the adhesive being used. Using super glue or other strong textile adhesives can work, but one foolproof way of ensuring the seam will not open is to stitch it together. This is particularly helpful if a thick fabric has been used, such as wool or velvet.

Slip Stitching the Outside Seam

Slip stitch is used to attach trims to traditional hand sewn lampshades. However, you can also use it to sew the seams of hard shades. For thicker fabrics such as wool it is ideal, as it stops the seam coming apart. The beauty of slip stitch is that the thread is slipped along the seam and the stitches themselves are invisible. Follow the 'Slip Stitch' tutorial in Chapter 4.

Closing the Inside Seam

Sometimes the seam inside the lampshade can gape open, especially if it has been made with double-sided laminate or a thicker laminate such as one of the metallic ones. The gap can be closed by adding a strip of bias binding, a length of matching fabric, or a piece of the laminate itself on the inside of the seam.

Slip stitching the seam of a hard lampshade where wool or other thick fabric has been used will ensure the seam stays closed. Using a curved needle on a seam with a pronounced curve, such as on this oval lampshade, really aids the process.

Emma Rockman at Rock Paper Scissor Shades: Bronze Blue Bees, 20cm drum lampshade. Emma uses matching colour trims on the inside seams of her hard lampshades, both as a design feature and to avoid any potential gaping seams.

PART 2
SOFT FABRIC LAMPSHADES

Soft fabric lampshades are made in an entirely different way from hard lampshades – they are hand sewn, with fabric worked and attached around a complete full frame. From the stretched fabric tailored lampshade to gathered, knife and box pleated, there are many styles to learn to make, and many options in sizes and shapes of frames.

Soft fabric lampshades do not have to be lined – there are advantages and disadvantages. If you do decide to line your lampshade, there is a choice of stretched 'balloon' linings, gathered linings, or pleated linings – the guide and tuition for these is included in Chapter 4. Lampshade frames are available in a range of shapes and sizes, and you can also get bespoke shapes and sizes made by a frame maker, including them remaking vintage favourites you may come across. It is always good to recycle, and lovely old lampshade frames are to be found in charity shops, on vintage sellers' websites, and at auction houses – they can be stripped and remade with new or vintage fabrics; there is tuition on repurposing lampshades in Chapter 7. To add further interest to lampshades, they can be embellished with a wide variety of trims. In Chapter 8 you will learn to make different styles that will partner the lampshade you have made, either the same outer fabric or another contrasting design to really make it sing.

Soft fabric lampshades take time and patience to make, as traditional hand sewing methods are used – you need to have, or intend to have, a love of hand sewing! However, it is a rewarding traditional craft to learn, and indeed a skill to gain. By working through the tutorials in Part 2 of this book, you will start with the basics and end by making complex and wonderful lampshades for your home, to a highly professional level.

Traditional tailored lampshades are made using a bowed empire frame, and are brought up to date in style with modern fabrics and trims. Lampshade made by Jane Warren for Clothkits workshops.

◀ Designer Melina Blaxland-Horne of Melodi Horne produces statement-piece lampshades in a variety of rich and vibrant colours in handwoven or in-house designed fabrics. They are complemented by their trademark coloured linen linings (PHOTO: TIM BEDDOW).

MATERIALS AND TECHNIQUES

There is a wide range of materials available for making soft lampshades – frames, linings, binding tapes, as well as the outer fabrics. This chapter guides you on which to use, and the techniques needed to create your own hand sewn lampshades.

MATERIALS

The following materials are needed to make soft fabric lampshades.

Frames

There are many different shapes and styles of lampshade frames, from the simple true drum to a complex frame that is bowed, has a scalloped base and top rings. They can be really small for chandeliers to very large for standard lamps and for ceilings in larger rooms.

The frames are made using steel wire and are powder coated in white paint, to prevent rust. They are constructed with a top ring and a base ring, which are connected by vertical metal rods called 'struts'. Frames have different numbers of struts – the larger the frame the more struts there are for strength.

The frames have a light fitting that is attached to the frame by gimbals – two metal 'arms' that usually go from the top ring down to the light fitting, although they can be positioned from the base ring too. They can be fixed or moveable (perfect for slanting the lampshade to aid reading – often called a reverse gimbal fitting). This light fitting is then positioned onto the lampshade base, into which you fit the light bulb. Small, usually chandelier or wall light frames, including half frames, most often have a candle-clip light fitting.

The gimbals can also hold a larger circular duplex fitting, which is positioned from the top ring, and has two uses: allowing the lampshade to be used either as a ceiling pendant or as a desk or standard lamp (*see* Chapter 1 for detail and fittings). Note that lampshade frames are often manufactured in imperial sizes (inches), and relate to the base ring diameter measurement.

Soft fabric lampshades can be made in a wide variety of styles and shapes using different fabrics and lining materials. Gathered lampshade made by Jane Warren.

Elements of a lampshade frame:

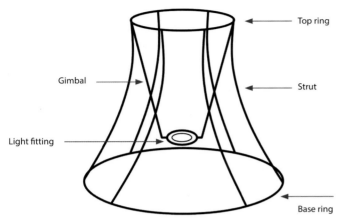

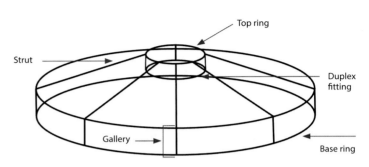

A traditional bowed empire lampshade frame with drop-down gimbal fitting.

A wide tiffany lampshade frame with duplex fitting.

There are many frame shapes available, here are some of the most popular:

Empire – straight sided, the top ring half the diameter of the base ring.

French drum – straight sided, the top ring smaller than the base, but marginally so.

Bowed empire – an empire with vertical struts bowed inwards.

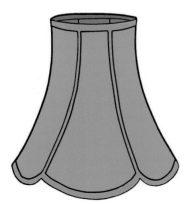

Bowed empire with scallop base ring – sometimes scalloped around the top ring too.

Collared empire – the empire (either plain or scalloped base) has two rings around the top.

Bowed empire with gallery – a bowed empire with a double ring around the base.

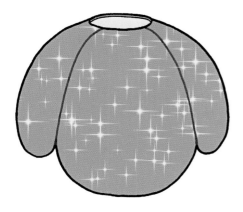

Scalloped tiffany or parachute – a rounded frame with outward curved struts.

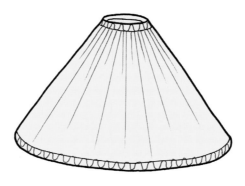

A cone or coolie – where the top ring is usually one third the diameter of the base ring.

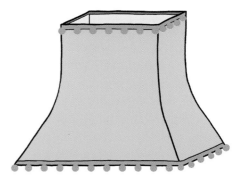

Pagoda – these are square or rectangular frames but with bowed corner struts.

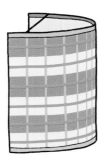

Half frame – usually small and placed onto wall light fittings; they can come in different shapes.

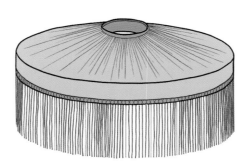

Wide tiffany – these shallow, wide frames have a duplex fitting.

Crown top – these come in two sections, the covers made separately and then connected together.

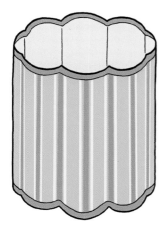

Daisy – either drums (that is, top and base ring the same size) or empires, they have curves in the rings coming outwards.

As well as those illustrated, there are lots of other frame shapes, such as bell, oval, square, rectangular, rectangular with cut corners, straight empires with collars, reverse scalloped frames, bowed drums, canister drums (where the top diameter is only just smaller than the base diameter), as well as straight drums.

Frame Sizes and Proportions

It is possible to buy lampshade frames in all different shapes and sizes, and order bespoke designs from a frame maker. Note that full frames are still ordered from manufacturers using imperial sizes, which relate to the base ring diameter. However, they are readily available in key generic sizes, taking into account the proportions needed to both make the frame itself as well as being pleasing to the eye.

FRAME SIZES AND PROPORTIONS

French drum frames		
Base diameter	Top diameter	Slope height
8in/20.5cm	6in/15.5cm	6in/15.5cm
10in/25.5cm	7in/18cm	7in/18cm
12in/30.5cm	8in/20.5cm	7.5in/19cm
14in/35.5cm	9in/23cm	8.5in/22cm
16in/40.5cm	10in/25.5cm	10in/25.5cm
18in/45.5cm	12in/30.5cm	12in/30.5cm

Empire frames		
Base diameter	Top diameter	Slope height
8in/20.5cm	4in/10cm	6in/15.5cm
10in/25.5cm	5in/13cm	7in/18cm
12in/30.5cm	6in/15.5cm	8in/20.5cm
14in/35.5cm	7in/18cm	8.5in/22cm
16in/40.5cm	8in/20.5cm	10in/25.5cm
18in/45.5cm	9in/23cm	10.5in/27cm

Bowed empire plain and bowed scallop base frames		
Base diameter	Top diameter	Slope height
8in/20.5cm	4in/10cm	7in/18cm
10in/25.5cm	5in/13cm	8in/20.5cm
12in/30.5cms	6in/15.5cm	9.5in/24cm
14in/35.5cm	7in/18cm	10.5in/27cm
16in/40.5cm	8in/20.5cm	13in/33cm
18in/45.5cm	9in/23cm	14.5in/37cm

Notes: The slope height is different from the vertical height, being slightly longer.

Sizes are approximate and correct at time of publication.

The fittings are usually either a drop-down gimbal fitting, with UK or EU fitting, or a duplex fitting.

Imperial to metric conversions are approximate (that is, not to exact millimetre).

Hand Sewn Lampshade Making Materials

As well as the lampshade frame, you will also need the following materials:

- lampshade tape (sometimes called India tape), 12mm wide – this is a woven tape, either bleached white or unbleached, that has no stretch
- thread – Terko or other thick thread is preferable to cotton, which can snap easily
- lining fabric – *see* the 'Lining Fabrics' section later in this chapter
- two short lengths of ribbon (or other to make your gimbal covers)
- scissors – you will need good-quality fabric scissors, large and small
- rotary cutter if preferred, for cutting lengths of fabric
- tracing or baking paper – this is used to place on top of a Lycra balloon lining when machine sewing the seams – white is best to see through

Gather the required materials together; you will also need a sewing machine if making a balloon lining for your lampshade.

- needle grabbers are made out of silicone and offer a sturdy grip on needles while sewing, or a needle gripper – which is like scissors but has gripper teeth to take hold of needles – helps too
- needles – long, strong, straight needles are good, or regular darners
- curved needle for adding bias binding around the rings
- pins – there are three types, choose the one you prefer working with:
  - Lils – very short pins made from nickel-plated steel, used also for sequin or bead work; usually 13mm long
  - appliqué pins – these are easier to use as they are longer at 20mm; they have a white polyester head on a steel pin
  - dressmaker pins – longer still, 30mm, made from hardened and polished steel
- pencils, or tailor's chalk or sewing chalk for dark fabric
- grid rule – these come in both metric and imperial sizes; choose one with a 45 degree marker
- waxy glue, such as Pritt, to help embed the stitches made.

You will also need a sewing machine for making balloon linings, and traditional tailored lampshades. Suggested suppliers for the materials are listed at the end of the book.

Fabrics

There are many fabrics to choose from to make hand sewn lampshades.

- For traditional tailored lampshades – silks, faux silks, cottons, polycottons, wools, and linens all work well; it helps if they have stretch on the 'bias' (*see* the 'What Is Meant by the "Bias" or the "Cross"?' section).
- You can use velvets but they allow very little light to filter through when lit.
- Be wary of reusing some fabrics or using vintage fabrics – some can be weak due to their age, and when pulled on the bias can split open. Try a small sample before committing.
- For gathered lampshades, the finer the fabric the better, for example Indian block prints, lawns, thin cottons, polycottons such as quilting fabrics, fine silks, and chiffon. Thicker fabrics such as linens can create bulk and bulge when gathered, and are hard on the hands to work with too.

- For knife pleated and box pleated lampshades, use silks, cottons, and linens with a good structure so that crisp pleats can be created.
- For sunray, fan pleated, and swathed lampshades, use silks, chiffon, and thinner fabrics, which are easy to handle.
- Fabrics that tend not to work are: stretchy fabrics such as jersey, as they will be pulled so much they will lose form; embroidered fabrics, as the fabric may be too tight to be tailored.

What Is Meant by the 'Bias' or the 'Cross'?
Fabrics are created by weaving threads in two directions – on the weft (horizontally) and the warp (vertically). Fabric has the selvedge (finished) edges running up vertically on both the left- and right-hand sides – this is the fabric being positioned on 'the straight'. Sometimes the selvedge is a printed section with the fabric house's name and colour details, or some have a simple edging or a run of pin holes where the fabric has been attached when being printed. Using fabric on 'the straight' of grain means you are handling it either from side to side (horizontally) or from top to base (vertically), and it does not stretch.

In traditional lampshade making, fabric is often used on the 'bias' or the 'cross'. This is achieved by turning it at a 45-degree angle so that it stretches, and this allows us to truly tailor the fabric for a good fit, especially on a curved frame. Different fabrics have different degrees of stretch, so it is worth checking before you buy or start using the fabric: turn the fabric from its straight position by 45 degrees, or corner to corner, give it a little pull, and you will discover if it is suitable. (*See* 'How to Find the Bias of your Fabric' on the following page.)

Fabric Pattern, Colour, and Texture
There are many designs and types of fabric to use, but consider these points when making your selection.

For traditional stretched soft lampshades:

- As these are often made using a bowed frame, fabric is mainly used on the bias for a perfect fit, so consider the design: a fabric with an animal print may mean the animals are positioned walking diagonally across the lampshade.

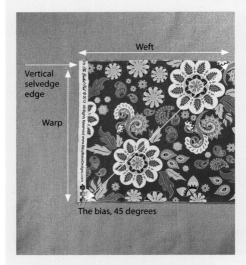

Place your choice of ironed fabric on the table, with the selvedge positioned vertically – this is the fabric being on 'the straight' of grain. There are two ways of finding the bias.

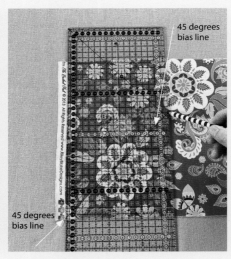

1. Using a grid ruler: these come with pre-printed 45-degree lines. Place the rule in line with the vertical selvedge edge. Position a pencil mark at each end of the 45-degree line. You can then join these by drawing a pencil line to connect them. Grid ruler by Creative Grids (UK).

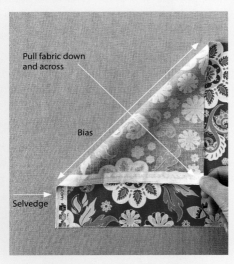

2. By hand: take one top corner edge of the fabric and pull it down and across, so that the selvedge-printed edge becomes parallel to the horizontal base line of the fabric. The angle achieved at the top is now 45 degrees and is the bias line to use.

- However, it is possible to make your lampshade with the fabric on the straight – *see* Chapter 5 for instruction.
- When using patterned fabrics, consider where you wish the main feature to be. For example, if the design has a large flower, position it centrally – having one on each side of the lampshade looks best.
- Because the covers of traditional stretched lampshades are made in two pieces, it is hard to pattern match the side seams, but there are tips on this in the tutorial also in Chapter 5.
- Hand embroidered fabric is difficult to stretch due to the close stitching, and the design can be lost and back stitching can show when the shade is lit. In these cases, consider embroidering it after you have made a plain covered lampshade, and use a thick lining to hide the work and maintain the pattern.

For gathered and pleated lampshades:

- Although these are made with the fabric on the straight, the pattern on an intricately designed fabric will become hidden as the fabric is pushed together. If you wish to see

Gathering the fabric loosely will reveal more of the pattern, which you may still want to see.

more of the design, use a loose gather, such as 1.5 × the circumference, so more will be visible.
- Lightweight fabrics are ideal for gathered lampshades as they can be gathered more easily and will let more light through once lit. Heavier fabrics may bunch up.
- You can also gather thinner fabrics more tightly with designs such as horizontal stripes, which will give a lovely effect.

In all cases, try samples of the fabrics you wish to use – gather and hold them up against a lit bulb, either with or without lining fabric. This will give you an idea of the end result, before you spend time making the lampshade and money on the fabric itself.

Lining Fabrics

Select the lining fabric in relation to the type of lampshade you are making, but also be mindful of the colour of the light that will be reflected. White can be harsh, whereas cream is warmer; a bright colour can pop but others can look a bit murky when lit. Try samples before making the lampshade.

Traditional Tailored Lampshades

Smooth balloon linings are usually made for traditional soft lampshades, especially if the frame is bowed, using the following fabrics:

- 4-way stretch Lycra – this is easy to use, does not fray or ladder, comes in an array of colours, is not expensive to buy, and gives a good professional look. Thicker Lycras used for dancewear are a good choice.
- Silk, crêpe-backed satin, linen, or cotton – these must be tailored to fit by handling the fabric on the bias, unless you use a linen mix (with Lycra), for example.
- Alternatively, consider having a designed patterned fabric balloon lining inside your lampshade (these look particularly good with a plain outer fabric), again made with the fabric on the bias.

Gathered or Pleated Lampshades

Either balloon linings or gathered or pleated fabric linings are made for these, using:

- 4-way stretch Lycra and so on, as in the previous list
- Silks, linens, or cottons for gathered or pleated linings for gathered or pleated lampshades. Using a crêpe-backed satin for thicker luxury or habotai for a thinner silk both work well. Gathered or pleated linings are made with the fabric on the straight – *see* the tutorial in the 'How to Make Gathered and Pleated Linings' section later in this chapter.

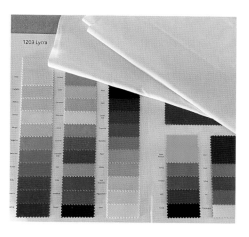

Lycra four-way stretch comes in a wide range of colours; this is from DSI London, a dancewear company, and is perfect for making balloon linings.

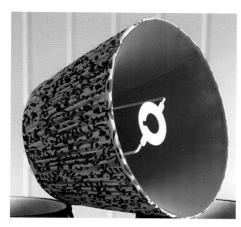

This gathered lampshade has been made with a 4-way stretch Lycra balloon lining in blue, making it the feature of the lampshade (made by Jane Warren).

Consider having a balloon lining using designer fabric (such as this Liberty fabric) inside your lampshade, adding interest to a plain outer fabric. Lampshade made by Jane Warren.

KEY TECHNIQUES

In order to make soft lampshades to a high standard, first learn the key techniques required: how to bind the frame, make linings, the outer fabric covers, and the stitches needed to hand sew onto the frame, followed by adding the finishing trims. These are the foundations of making traditional hand sewn lampshades.

There are two key types of traditional lampshade:

- tailored, where fabric is stretched tight across a frame and hand sewn into position
- gathered and pleated, where the fabric is fashioned into formal pleats or relaxed gathers and hand sewn into place.

In addition, there are lots of other styles to make. Having mastered these techniques, you will be able to go on to make them too.

Order of Work

For making hand sewn lampshades, the order of work is:

1. binding the lampshade frame
2. if lining the lampshade with a balloon lining, making the lining
3. making the outer cover
4. sewing the outer cover onto the frame
5. inserting and sewing a balloon lining onto the frame
6. if having a gathered lining, making and sewing it onto the frame
7. making and adding gimbal covers or 'neateners'
8. trimming/completing your lampshade.

Note that for pleated lampshades, the lining is often positioned in advance of the outer cover – *see* Chapter 6 for details.

The lampshade tape should be wrapped tightly over the rings at a wide angle, just covering the previous one.

Binding the Lampshade Frame

In order to start making tailored lampshades using traditional methods, the frame is first bound with lampshade tape. The outer cover and lining will be sewn into this and therefore it needs to be robust and non-stretchy, and bound very tightly onto the frame. The tape comes in large rolls or by the metre from suppliers. The 12mm size suits most sizes of frame.

You will:

- Bind the top ring and the base ring; the fabric cover and lining will be sewn into them.
- Bind two opposite side struts – these are temporary bindings, and are needed if making a stretched tailored cover and a balloon lining – the tape will be removed after these have been made.
- Cut lengths of tape 2.5 × the circumferences of your top and base ring, and 2.5 × the height of the two struts.

The following tuition is based on a right-handed person binding the frame and moving in an anti-clockwise route around the frame. Please reverse (that is, start on the right of a strut and move in a clockwise direction) if you prefer – you will have the same result.

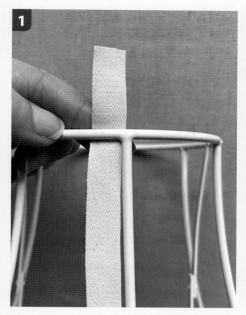

Starting with the top ring, with your left hand, place one end of the tape to the left of a strut, behind the ring, leaving a spare 4cm 'tail' at the top.

Now bring this tail end over and in front of the ring, to the right of the strut, and wrap it around the top ring to the right, keeping it smooth and with a wide angle. Keep this tail end in place with your right hand.

Using your left hand, place the long tape on the left, over the front of the ring, going over the wrapped tape on the ring, and wrap it over the tail end. Once the tail is covered, pull the tape firmly, keeping it smooth.

Continued on the following page.

TOP TIPS FOR EXCELLENT BINDING

- Ensure the binding is really tight – any movement means your cover will become baggy too.
- Wrap the frame *just* covering the previous wrap, at about a 45-degree angle. This will avoid bulk and keep the ring smooth.
- When you meet a strut, do a wide-angled wrap over it, and then just after that one, do one wrap straight over – it will perfectly hide the metal with no bulk around the strut.
- If the tape wrinkles or gathers, use your nail to smooth it out.
- From time to time as you go round, check the tape is really tight and, if it is not, go back and re-tighten or re-wrap.
- Start the binding at a strut near the gimbal; the seams of the outer cover will be positioned in the same place.
- If you are wrapping a large frame, tie your tape up into a ball with an elastic band. It will be easier to wrap around instead of having a really long piece flapping around you.

When binding a large frame with tape, tie the tape in a rubber band for ease, instead of having a long length to hold and wrap.

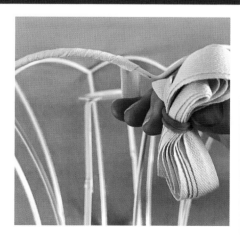

4 At a good wide angle, continue to wrap around the top ring, keeping it as smooth as possible, each one just covering the last. This will ensure there is no bulk.

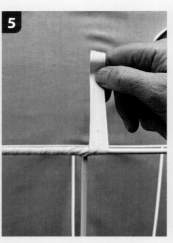

5 When you reach a strut or the gimbal, make a wide wrap over it, and then when past the strut or gimbal, do one straight wrap upwards; this will cover the metal and you will not have bulk either. Keep the tension, pulling as you go around.

6 When you near the end, raise up the length of the tape into a loop with your left hand and, not lessening the tension, place the tail end over to the right of the strut.

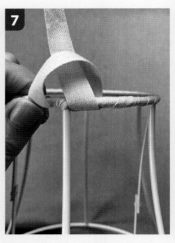

7 Then with your right hand, bring the end of the tape, which is on the right, upwards and feed it through the loop. Keep it tightly pulled.

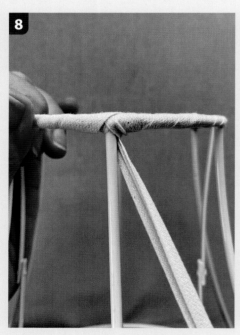

8 Make a flat knot, removing any gathers or puckers with your fingernail, and pull it down really tight.

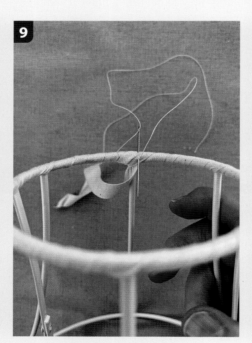

9 Make a few simple small stitches, ensuring the needle goes through all layers of the tape; knot and cut away the end of the thread.

10 Then cut away the excess tape to the stitches. Repeat around the base ring, starting at the same strut.

Now bind the side struts, following these steps:

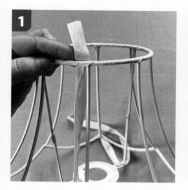

1 With your left hand, place one end of the tape to the left of a strut, behind the ring, leaving around 5cm spare at the top.

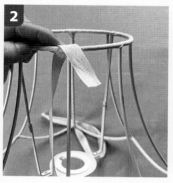

2 Bring it over the top ring and down to the right of the strut.

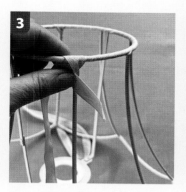

3 Now take it behind the strut to the left and bring it over the front to the right.

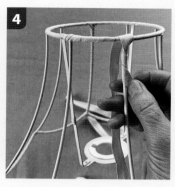

4 Wrap the tail end down and around the strut, ensuring it is flat and just covers the last wrap.

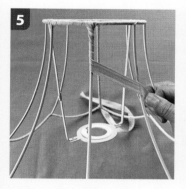

5 Now bring the long piece on the left over to the right and cover the already wrapped tail-end tape. Once it is covered, pull the tape down tight.

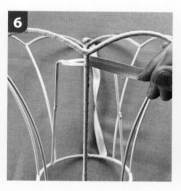

6 Wrap at a wide angle, just covering the last piece, all the way down to the base of the strut

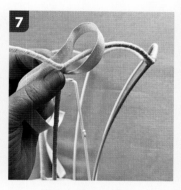

7 Now make a loop, bringing the tape from the right front to the back and left of the strut.

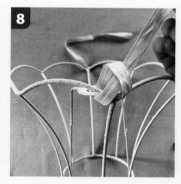

8 Bring the tape to the front left of the strut and tuck the end through this loop, not letting go of any tension.

Pull the tape through as flat as you can and make a knot, pulling down the tape so that it is tight and as smooth as possible. Now repeat for the opposite strut.

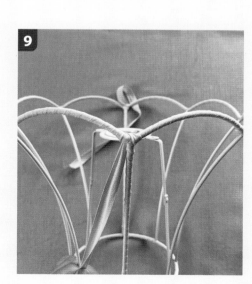

The tape will be removed from the two opposite side struts after the lining and cover have been made, so keep the excess tape or tails so it is easier to remove. The frame is now ready to work on.

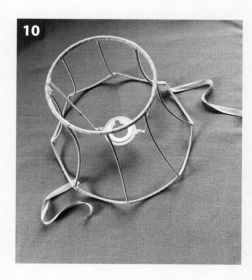

Lampshade Linings

Choosing Whether to Line or Not Line Your Lampshade
The advantages of lining are:

- All the metalware inside and the struts will be hidden from view.
- The light transmitted will be softened, as it will emit the colour of the lining, not the fabric choice.
- The bulb will not be visible from the outside when lit.
- Lining will protect the fabric from dust inside.

The advantages of not lining are:

- The main advantage of not lining a lampshade is that it will only take half the time to make!
- If you are using thick fabric, such as a wool or velvet, there will not be the issue of the bulb being seen.
- The colour of your chosen outer fabric will be the light you have in the room, and you may prefer to have this pop of colour.
- With ceiling/pendant lampshades, you look up into the fabric pattern as opposed to a plain lining; the metal struts can be paint sprayed a bright colour to make them a feature.

Both styles will be completed with a bias binding trim to hide the stitches; a wider bias binding is used to hide the lampshade tape for unlined lampshades.

This unlined lampshade has been made using a thick barkcloth fabric, and the frame inside paint sprayed bright red as a feature. Lampshade by Jane Warren.

Types of Linings

Balloon Lining
This smooth, stretched lining is placed inside the lampshade frame. It is hand sewn around the top and base rings, and 'balloons' away slightly from the metalware inside, hiding the struts. It is made in two sections for a perfect fit (although square and rectangular frames may need four sections). They are usually fitted after the outer cover has been sewn in place (but are made first).

External Lining or an Interlining
This type of lining is placed on the outside of the frame and is an undercover for the main outer fabric. This is needed when a really thin fabric, such as chiffon, is being used (they can have an additional balloon lining if required). External linings and interlinings are also used for sectional lampshades where a balloon lining cannot be fitted, or for very small candle lampshades. They are made using the same method as making a balloon lining, or can be sewn directly onto the struts.

WHAT IS A HANDLING ALLOWANCE?

When positioning the lining and fabric onto the frame, you will need an extra amount of fabric all around – this is called the 'handling allowance', sometimes referred to as the 'working allowance'. It is required because you hold onto and pull the fabric to achieve the correct tension and tailoring to make your lampshade. When working out how much fabric you need, add on the amount you like working with as a handling allowance (usually 3–6cm) all around, for each piece you use. If you wish to use the allowance as your bias trim for non-lined lampshades (*see* tuition in Chapter 5), allow 6cm.

The handling allowance is held onto when pulling and pinning the fabric for a perfect tailored fit.

Gathered or Pleated Linings

These are made and fitted either after the outer cover has been sewn in place or beforehand. However, for knife pleated and box pleated lampshades, it is best they are sewn in position first, as otherwise the outer tailored pleats can get pulled out of place and shape. They can be full gathered or pleated or semi-gathered/semi-pleated.

How to Make a Balloon Lining

The Process

The lining is made on one half of the outside of the bound frame, in two equal pieces of fabric that are then machine sewn together, with opposite side seams. The lining is then positioned inside the frame and hand sewn in place. For smaller to medium-size frames, the Lycra fabric can be doubled over into one workable piece, but with other non-stretch fabrics (worked on the bias) or with larger frames, just use one piece of lining fabric. This will then be matched with another separate piece. There is also extra fabric needed as a handling allowance – this will be held onto when the fabric is stretched and pinned in place on the frame. The balloon lining in the tutorial is made using 4-way stretch Lycra, and therefore it does not need to be made on the bias.

First Steps

1. Bind the top and base rings and two opposite side struts of the frame with lampshade tape.
2. Measure and cut enough fabric to go around the whole frame, plus the extra for the handling allowances – this will be doubled over (or if you have a large frame, cut two separate pieces plus the handling allowance). Follow the tutorial to make balloon lining.

TUTORIAL: HOW TO MAKE A BALLOON LINING

The materials needed to make balloon lining are: a length of lining; a box of pins; a pencil; tailor's chalk; scissors; tracing paper (white); a sewing machine; matching colour thread to the lining.

Fold the lining, right sides together, in half. Place it around half of the frame and pin it at the four 'corners' of the half of the frame (where the bound side struts meet the top and base rings); pin it into the tape, leaving the handling allowance free all around. It can be loosely attached at this stage. Ensure the sharps of the pins are facing inwards.

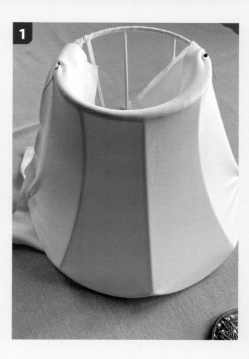

Continued on the following page.

2

Now, working in a clockwise direction, add pins where the struts meet the rings – around the top ring, then two down the side strut, then along the base ring, and then up the second side strut. As you pin, pull the fabric in a little to tighten (but not too tight at this stage).

3

Carry on around the frame in a clockwork direction, stretching the lining to tighten the fabric, adding a few more pins. Remove pins already in place and then pull and re-pin; go around again, pinning and tightening, ending with the pins around 1cm apart. The fabric should be taut but still with some 'give'.

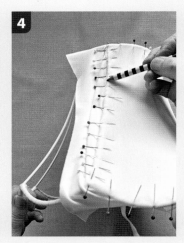

4

Using a pencil, draw a line on the lining down the vertical side struts, being careful to position the mark on the middle of the strut line only, not inside it. Repeat for the opposite side. If you are using dark fabric for the lining, use tailor's chalk.

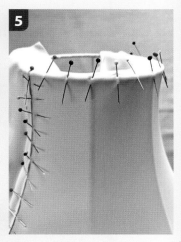

5

Where the vertical struts meet the top and base rings, place a small dot (see blue dot in image) using tailor's chalk or another removeable marker (permanent marks such as pencil will be seen on the lining). Alternatively, small stickers or tailor's tacks can be used. This will show the position of where to pin in the lining when it is time to insert it.

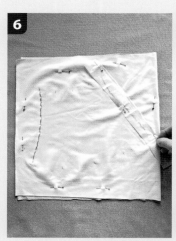

6

Unpin the lining off the frame, lay it down flat, and add a few pins around to keep the two pieces together (however if you have made the lining using one piece of fabric, now match it to another piece, right sides together). Add strips of tracing paper over the pencil lines, ensuring it is positioned 4cm higher and lower than the lines. Do not worry if your pencil lines are wiggly – it is the nature of the fabric.

7

Thread your sewing machine with thread that matches the colour of the lining fabric. Place the lining on the sewing machine, ready to start sewing 4cm higher than, and just 2–3mm inside, the pencil lines – not following the wiggles but in a consistent line! Now machine stitch regular-sized stitches and tension, downwards through the paper, and carry on 4cm longer than the pencil lines. Machine stitch each side twice for strength.

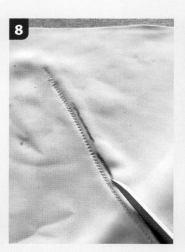

8

Remove the tracing or baking paper by holding the two sides of it together and pulling carefully downwards. As it is perforated, it should come away easily, but if fragments remain, use a pin to remove them. Carefully trim away the excess lining fabric along the seams, between the sewn seam and the pencil line, leaving a 2–3mm seam allowance. This will ensure that the seam will be not seen when positioned behind a strut.

9

Trim around the top and base edges, keeping 4–5cm above and below your dots for the handling allowance. Shape the edges so they match the curve of the frame. Do not worry if it is not symmetrical; it has been tailored to fit. Put a pin into the dots you have marked around the rings, so that it goes through to the other side; add dots there too so they are on both sides – this will create the pattern for where the lining will be placed once you are ready to insert it.

Instructions for inserting the balloon lining are included in Chapter 5.

Balloon Lining – Non-Stretch Fabrics

Using non stretch fabrics for your lining will mean they will need to be made with the fabric on the bias. Follow the steps for making the outside cover of a traditional lampshade (Chapter 5, Steps 1–5) but then machine the lining seams 3mm inside the drawn seam pencil/chalk lines. You can then insert it following the steps in the 'Inserting a Balloon Lining' tutorial in Chapter 5. These patterned linings really suit lampshades with a plain outer cover, or if you have a large ceiling lampshade to look up into.

Linings made from non-stretch fabrics will need to be made on the bias, as this striped cotton balloon lining has been – carefully pattern matched at the seams.

How to Make Gathered and Pleated Linings

Gathered and pleated linings are made using just one length of fabric (or lengths of fabric) on the straight and are only usually made for straight-sided frames. Calculations are worked out in advance, so that the fabric amount is shared equally around the frame. The fabric is attached and hand sewn onto the outside of the base ring, and then pulled inside the frame and up to the top. It is then sewn in place, the stitches being on the front of the ring. If you want to pair these linings with gathered or pleated outer covers, check the final result by testing samples of both in front of a lit bulb, to avoid them looking too messy together. With a pleated cover, position your lining in first.

There are two key types of pleated and gathered linings:

- Full pleated/gathered – these are made using lining fabric that is either 1.5 or 2 × the base ring circumference, that is, it is pleated or gathered around both the base and top rings.
- Semi-pleated/gathered – these are made with the same measurement of fabric as the base circumference (plus 1cm each end for seams). They will closely fit around the base ring, with the fabric only gathered or pleated around the top ring.

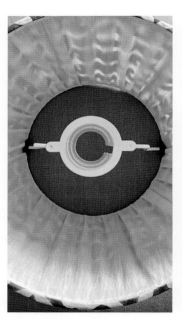

This gathered lampshade has a semi-pleated lining made using linen. The fabric fits exactly around the base ring and then soft pleats have been created around the top ring.

The Process

1. Choose if you wish to have a full or semi-gathered or pleated lining. Work out the amount of fabric required: it is going to be apportioned between the number of struts on the frame to ensure the fullness is shared around equally – remember that the top ring is often smaller than the base ring so fabric that has the perfect fullness around the base may look scrunched up around the top ring.

2. It helps to write down the maths needed for calculating the fabric quantities and the amount to be shared around the rings (*see* the calculation in the 'First Steps' section for an example).

3. These linings are made with fabric as a loose length, with no seams, and therefore it is not necessary to bind two opposite side struts with lampshade tape, just the top and base rings. Therefore you will not need a sewing machine.

First Steps

For the tutorial, a full gathered and pleated lining is made because there is not much difference in size between the top and base ring of the frame (*see* the semi-gathered/ pleated lining being made in the gathered lampshade tutorial in Chapter 6). Here are the calculations:

- The frame size (canister drum) is:
  - base ring 8in/20.5cm
  - top ring 7in/18cm
  - height 7in/18cm
  - fixed drop-down gimbal with UK/EU fitting.
- For the lining fabric quantity:
  - it will have × 1.5 fullness
  - the circumference of the 8in/20.5cm diameter base ring is 64.5cm (20.5 × pi 3.14 = 64.37; rounded up)
  - 1.5 (fullness) × 64.5 = 96.75
  - divide this amount by 6 (the number of struts) = 16.12, rounded down = 16cm; this is the amount of fabric that will be fitted between each of the six struts, both top and base rings.
- For cutting the fabric:
  - the calculated amount of fabric to cut is: 96cm (16cm × 6) plus 1cm for each end, which will be folded in so there are no raw edges = 98cm
  - the height needed is: the height of the frame (18cm) plus 3cm both top and base for a working or handling allowance = 24cm
  - therefore cut 98cm wide × 24cm high.

If there was to be a semi-gathered or semi-pleated lining for this 8in/20.5cm sized frame, the width cut would be the circumference of the base ring, plus 1cm for each end as folded seams – therefore 66.5cm (rounded up). The width of the fabric along the top would be divided into 6 (number of struts), so 10.75cm; this would be the amount fitted between the top struts, either gathered or pleated.

If you are making a lining for a larger frame, you will not get the amount of fabric needed from one width. Therefore, cut two equal widths of fabric, each worked over half the frame. It is not necessary to machine join the lengths, to avoid bulk. Simply divide the full amount you need by 2 and add on 1cm to each end. Each section will start and end at a strut to help hide the metal. For larger frames, use three equal-cut widths, and so on.

If you are having a gathered lining, please refer to the 'Gathering Fabric Methods' section later in this chapter.

The completed full gathered lining, positioned in place before its outer cover, using crêpe-backed satin. Follow the steps below to make this lining.

TUTORIAL: HOW TO MAKE GATHERED AND PLEATED LININGS

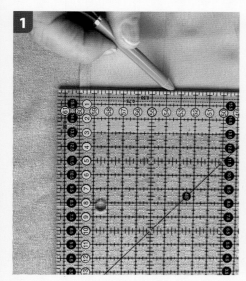

1 Cut the ironed fabric to the required size – this is 98cm wide × 24cm high. The fabric, crêpe-backed satin, is slippery; using a rotary cutter helps. Lay the fabric on a table, face (right) side down. This lampshade will have the shiny side of the satin inside, so the matt side is seen here. Now draw a line along the base horizontal edge of the fabric, 3cm up from the base edge. This is where it will be gathered.

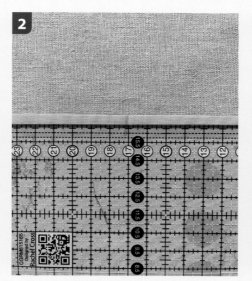

2 Place pencil/chalk marks along the top and base horizontal edges of the fabric, within the 3cm allowance. This is to show the apportioning of the fabric between the six struts; these are every 16cm. Allow 1cm at each end for turnings, so the first mark will be 17cm along. Press or iron this 1cm inwards, that is, folded towards you.

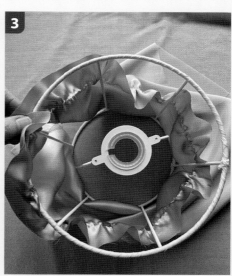

3 Gather the fabric, either on the sewing machine or by hand using running stitch (*see* 'Gathering-Fabric Methods' after this tutorial), and pull the threads so that the panel is approximately the right size to fit around the base ring. This fabric has a shiny side, which we want to have as the inside lining, so place it face (right) side down.

Continued on the following page.

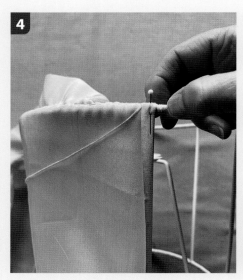

4 Place the frame on your table with the base upwards. Place the fabric face down, and pin the base edge of it where the gathers are. The 1cm edge should be turning towards you. Pin this, face down, to the taped frame, starting at a strut – the one where you started/ended the taping.

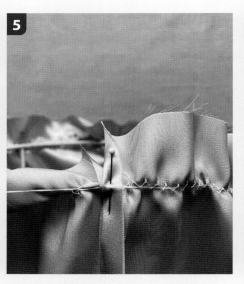

5 Now attach the rest of the lining by pairing your pencil- or chalk-drawn marks on the fabric to each of the six struts. Pin it in place to the bound ring at these points, ensuring that the pin goes behind the gathering threads so they are free to be pulled. When you reach the end, fold over the 1cm cut edge towards you so it lays on top of the first turned 1cm edge, and pin in place, again leaving the gathering threads free.

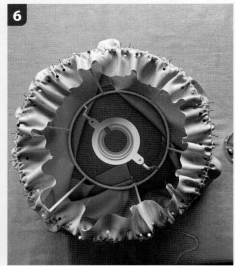

6 Take hold of the threads and pull gently so the fabric gathers around the frame – just taut enough so it fits snugly around the ring. Between the struts, share out the gathers so that they are uniform and pin them around the taped ring. The pins will need to be around 1cm apart. Now hand sew the lining in place using small streetly stitches (see 'Streetly Stitch' tuition later in this chapter) on the front of the ring.

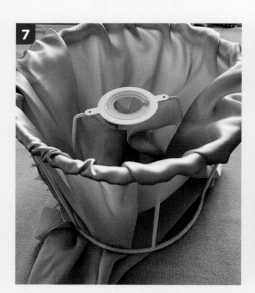

7 After sewing, trim the excess fabric to the stitches, being really careful not to snip into them. If you have a fraying fabric, use Pritt Stick glue on the stitches. Now turn the lining inside into the frame, pulling it upwards. This will hide your base ring stitching. Pull the fabric up taut and pin in the two folded 1cm turnings. Working around the ring, now match the pencil/chalk marks to the relevant struts and pin in place.

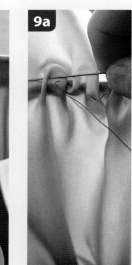

8 Using sharp scissors, snip into the fabric down and around the gimbals so that it fits around them, ensuring there is no gap at the base. You do not need to add gimbal covers for gathered linings as the fabric-cut edges can be turned inwards. Pin the lining around either side of the gimbal.

9 You can now gather the fabric into place, either by placing running stitch around the top (in front of the top ring) or fashioning it by hand, and then pulling the threads. Alternatively you can hand pleat the excess fabric; this is usually done by eye. Trim away any excess fabric, adding Pritt Stick if it is liable to fray.

Gathering Fabric Methods

There are two methods of gathering lining or outer-cover fabric in advance of it being attached to the frame – one is on a sewing machine and the other is by hand. You can also gather or pleat the lining by hand after it has been pinned in position onto the frame. For linings, it is best to gather the fabric for the base (using either a machine or by hand), attach it to the frame, and then hand gather the top; this way you will be able to control the gathers more, and it is a must if you wish to have a pleated top lining. To make the outer fabric covers, you can also follow this method, or choose to machine both the top and base edges of the fabric. Work out which methods work best for you. The 'Sewing Machine' tutorial uses a zigzag-stitch method but it is possible to buy a gathering foot for sewing machines.

Sewing Machine

It is a good idea to try out this technique on a sample of fabric first.

1. Once you have apportioned the fabric into six equal parts (plus allowed 1cm at each end), draw a 3cm line along the base horizontal edge. This will be the sewing line.
2. Set your machine to have a wide, long zigzag stitch and place the fabric under the presser foot, 3cm up from the base edge (i.e. on your drawn line) and 1cm inwards.
3. Manually turn the hand wheel so that the needle goes down through the fabric and then upwards. When the needle reaches the top, lift up the presser foot. The two threads will be on the top of the fabric (the bobbin thread will be looped over the main thread), so gently get hold of them both and pull them towards you the length of the fabric.
4. Put down the presser foot, then while holding the threads in one hand, start the machine on a slow speed – the zigzags should go over the two threads you are holding. Make sure you sew along the marked 3cm line for accuracy.
5. Stop 1cm before the end and take the fabric off the machine, cutting the two threads to around 10cm long.
6. Now place the fabric on the table; gently pull these threads and gather until it is approximately the right size to fit around the base ring.
7. You can either repeat for the top ring or sew the gathers by hand or on the frame.

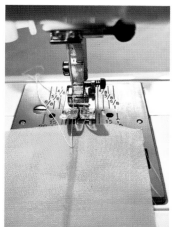
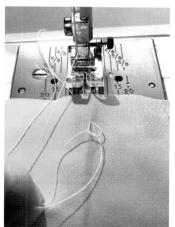
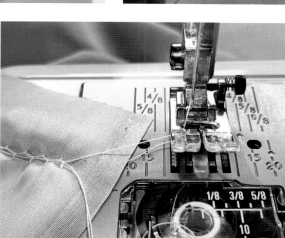

Using a zigzag stitch over the two threads on the sewing machine results in quick and easy fabric gathering. The fabric can then be shared around the frame.

Hand Gathering

You can also gather the fabric by hand sewing a simple running stitch.

1. Lay the fabric on the table, and as in the machine sewing instructions, apportion the fabric into six equal parts (marked in pencil or chalk).
2. Then simply use running stitch along the 3cm line drawn above the base of the fabric's horizontal edge.
3. You can have one long run of thread and gather at the end, or gather it as you sew along – then pull the thread/s at the end and gather to fit around the base ring.
4. You can repeat for the top ring or sew the gathers by hand on the frame.

Hand Gathering on the Frame

The lining can also be attached onto the frame, pinning it in place where the apportioned fabric meets the struts, and

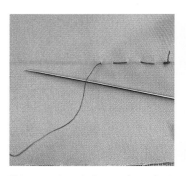 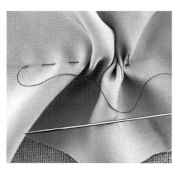

Using running stitch, sew along the 3cm horizontal line along the base of the fabric; at the end, pull the threads to gather.

An example of streetly stitch sewing the lining around the base of this Tiffany lampshade. It is always sewn on the front of the rings. These stitches will be covered by bias binding.

then gathered. Using a needle and thread, make running stitches just in front of the ring – this is featured in the previous 'Gathered and Pleated Linings' tutorial.

Stitches Used for Soft Lampshade Making

There are two key stitches used for lampshade making: 'streetly' (or lampshade) stitch and slip stitch. In addition, small running stitches are often used for attaching trims and gathering fabric.

Streetly Stitch

Streetly stitch was originally used by glove makers and was adopted by lampshade makers as it offers very secure interlocking stitches. It makes vertical stitches from the base to the top of the rings, as well as diagonally, linking them together; from the side they form a 'z' shape. It is used for hand sewing the outer covers and linings onto the frame, into the lampshade tape.

It is important that the stitches are situated on the front of the lampshade frame rings, as this way they will not be seen when looking down or up into a lampshade. The stitches are then hidden by adding a trim both around the top and base rings.

To best make your stitches:

*   Hold the frame either on your knee if you are using a large frame (although a tray or other is useful to protect yourself from the pins!), or on the table for smaller ones.
*   It does not matter if you stitch from top down to the base, or the opposite way, but it can help to stitch from the base of the ring upwards if you are working with your frame on a table, as that way you can pull the working allowance fabric up as you sew up, ensuring a lovely tight attachment.
*   You can work in either direction – to the right or to the left around the frame.
*   Use a darner needle with either polyester thread doubled (cotton can snap, as the thread is pulled tight for this stitch) or single thread if using thicker thread such as Terko satin.
*   For this tutorial, contrasting colour thread is used to show the steps, but in reality, use matching colour thread.

Now follow the tutorial steps to learn streetly stitch.

TUTORIAL: STREETLY STITCH

Streetly stitch is used to attach the cover to the lampshade frame, which will have been pinned into position (*see* tutorial). Take hold of the handling allowance with one hand at all times when sewing so that you do not lose the correct tension; then remove the first pin and place a knotted threaded needle at the base and on the front of the ring.

Push the needle in and into the lampshade tape, and vertically out at the top front of the ring. All stitches should be on the front of the ring, not the top or below. If it feels difficult to push through, wiggle the needle to help.

Take the needle back down to the start point and repeat the stitch (that is, in and up to the top again) in the same place. This strengthens the stitching.

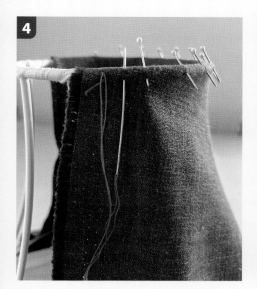

Now take the needle in a diagonal downwards direction, to the base of the ring, and put the needle in there (parallel to the first stitch along the base). These stitches are around 7mm wide.

Sew vertically upwards again, attaching the thread to the lampshade tape, and come out at the top of the ring, as before. The stitches should be the same size and come out parallel to the previous stitch.

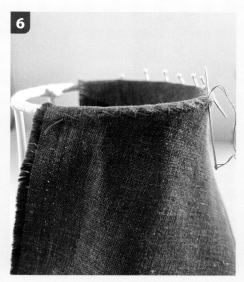

Take the needle down to the base again; go in and up to the top of the ring. This will create the first (sideways) 'z', then make the second diagonal stitch. Repeat the stitches all along. If you are sewing on your knee sideways, you will see the defined 'z'-shaped stitches. Knot the thread at the end.

Chapter 4 – Materials and Techniques   **93**

Slip Stitch

Slip stitch is so called because the thread is slipped along inside a seam (such as in the fold of bias binding) with tiny connecting stitches, and therefore the stitches and thread themselves are not seen. It is used to attach bias binding trim to a lampshade frame after the cover and linings have been sewn in place.

It is worth using a curved needle, as obviously the lampshade also has curved rings, but a good darning needle can be used too. Ideally, a matching thread should be used but for this tutorial a brighter thread has been used to clearly show the steps needed.

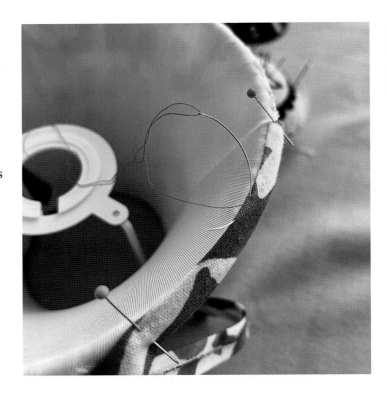

Using slip stitch to attach the bias binding trim onto the lampshade frame means invisible stitching. It helps to use a curved needle.

TUTORIAL: SLIP STITCH

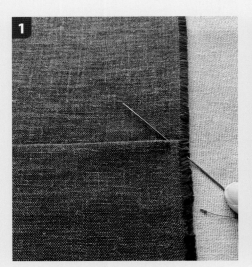

1 Thread a needle with single thread and knot one end. Put the needle underneath the folded edge (usually of bias binding) to hide the knot, and come out in the edge of the fold.

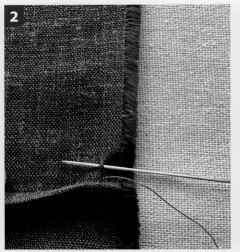

2 Then directly opposite where you have come out, pick up a couple of threads of the opposite lining fabric with the needle and pull the thread through.

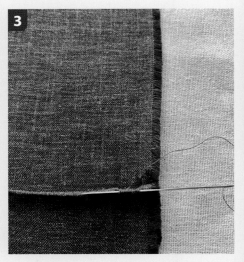

3 Take the needle back into the fabric, again directly opposite the lining stitches; put the needle into the fold of the bias binding and slip it along (around 1cm).

Now put the needle back into the lining, directly opposite where you have come out of the bias binding, and again simply pick up a couple of threads.

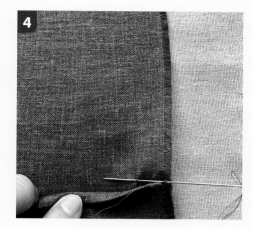

Repeat steps 1–4 by putting the needle back through into the bias, slipping the needle along its fold, then going back into the lining, collecting a couple of stitches, and so on.

Always pick up the threads and return directly opposite each other. Pull the threads and all the stitches will disappear.

Gimbal Covers or Neateners

When a lampshade is lined with a balloon lining, cuts are made into the fabric for it to fit around the gimbals, otherwise the lining will gather and bag around their raw cut edges. For this reason, gimbal covers are made. They can be made using different fabrics, including the lining fabric, the outer cover fabric, and a complementary or contrasting colour or silky ribbon (satin is best). You can decide on the size you wish to have in relation to the frame you are using, but around 10–12mm wide is the average, and cut around 6cm long. It is important that if not using ribbon (which has bound edges), the fabric used is folded under itself so that all raw edges are hidden.

See Chapter 5 on fitting balloon linings, adding gimbal covers, and adding the bias binding for your hand sewn lampshades.

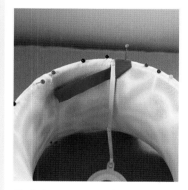

Gimbal covers are made using strips of fabric, folded over so that the raw cut edges are only on one side, and ironed into neat strips. These are then placed over the snipped cuts in balloon linings (*see* Chapter 5).

TRADITIONAL TAILORED LAMPSHADES

Traditional tailored lampshades have fabric stretched flat across the frame – usually on the bias for a perfect fit, as they are generally made using curved frames such as bowed empires. Like balloon linings, the covers are made on half of the frame, and joined together by machining the seams, although larger, square or rectangular, and other-shaped frames may need more sections for a perfect fit. These will be sewn directly onto the frame when being made (*see* the 'Sectional Lampshades' section later in this chapter).

When making these lampshades, extra fabric is allowed all around the cover as a 'handling allowance', enabling you to move and stretch the fabric as it is made and tailored to fit. They are then either left unlined or are lined usually with a balloon lining (*see* Chapter 4). The stitching is then hidden with a bias trim and choice of either bias or a more extravagant base trim (*see* Chapter 8 for making these).

FRAMES

A bowed empire frame is a classic shape and style that is chosen for the tutorial here. It can be made either with plain top and base rings or with a scalloped base ring. You can also use bell-shaped and other curved frames, as well as straight-sided empires (*see* Chapter 4 for frame shapes). However, if you wish to use a square, rectangular, or unusual-shaped frame, you will use the same method but will need to create more sections – *see* later in this chapter.

FABRIC QUANTITIES

To work out how much fabric you will need using a bowed empire frame with the fabric on the bias:

- For the width of the fabric, measure half way around the base ring of the frame (or half of the circumference, which is the diameter × pi (3.14), then divided by 2).
- For the height of the fabric, measure (on the outside of the frame) from one base ring strut to one exactly opposite (that is, half the frame) on the top ring.
- Add on a working allowance of 5cm all around. This will give you the size needed for one half of the cover – it will be made in two sections, so double this for both sides.

Alternatively, simply hold the fabric up against the frame on the bias and cut around, but allow for the handling allowance.

Note that if you wish to make your bias binding from the same top fabric, you will need to add this to the amount of fabric needed. You can join lengths of bias, or to use just one uncut length – *see* tutorial on making bias in Chapter 8.

Soft tailored lampshades have stretched and hand sewn covers on the frame, and can be decorated with hand made trims. Lampshade made by Jane Warren.

TEMPLATES OR PATTERNS

There is much pinning and stretching involved in making a stretched outer cover lampshade and it does take time. It is tempting to try to make a pattern to make covers for the same size lampshade to use in the future. However, this rarely works because every fabric behaves in a different way – they have a different stretch capacity, and each one needs to be individually fitted and tailored. That said, if you are making more than one lampshade using the same fabric, you can make a template or pattern by placing a sheet of greaseproof/baking paper over your made cover (before it is fitted onto the frame), tracing around it, indicating seam and ring/strut positions, and then using this as a pattern to make the next one.

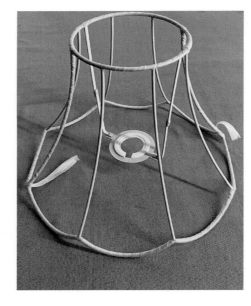

Getting started: bind the top and base rings of the frame permanently, and two opposite side struts temporarily, in preparation for making the lampshade.

ON THE STRAIGHT OR ON THE BIAS?

The best way to make fabric hug a frame is to make the cover with the fabric on the bias or the cross. This is because the fabric stretches so well at 45 degrees that it is possible to pin it precisely in position for the perfect tailoring needed. However, this means that a pattern may be lost; for example, animals will be walking diagonally across the lampshade, as opposed to across it, and stripes will be diagonal too (*see* Chapter 4 on how to find the bias of your fabric). That said, it is possible to make traditional lampshades with the fabric on 'the straight', but it is vital that the fit is perfect when pinned and tailored, as there is no 'give' to the fabric. Tutorials for both methods are included here.

You can also make balloon linings using fabrics on the bias instead of 4-way stretch Lycra as outlined in the tutorial in Chapter 4. You can follow the same method outlined here to make an outer cover, but for the lining, machine 3mm inside the pencil line, not on it, so that it fits inside the frame.

Making the Cover on the Bias
The tutorial here is for making a traditional stretched cover for a bowed scalloped empire frame with these specifications:

- base ring diameter 10in/25.5cm
- top-ring diameter 5in/13cm
- slope height to base of scallop 8½in/22cm, eight struts
- drop-down gimbal fitting, moveable arm.

The outer cover is made with the fabric on the bias, and in two sections. It is important that the grain line of the fabric is matched in the two pieces, as this will ensure a good fit. You can indicate this on the fabric in advance, by making arrow marks in chalk or pencil showing the fabric on 'the straight' or 'straight of grain' (*see* tutorial).

Getting Started – First Steps
1. Gather together the materials and haberdashery needed to make the lampshade (*see* Chapter 4), plus your chosen fabric.
2. If you wish to line your lampshade, make a balloon lining in advance of the cover, and put it to one side.
3. Bind the frame with lampshade tape around the top and base rings (permanently) and two opposite side struts (temporarily).

4. Place your ironed fabric onto the table, and cut one piece to size that will be placed on half of the frame (in this example, 40cm × 40cm). Draw matching arrows on both sides (face and reverse) of it – these indicate the fabric straight of grain (the vertical/warp direction).

5. You also need to draw the arrows on the second piece of fabric you will be using so they match in direction/grain to the first piece. It does not need to be cut to size at present as you may wish to pattern match at the seams.

Now you can start making the cover for the lampshade following the tutorial steps.

The completed traditional tailored lampshade with block printed fabric stretched across and sewn onto the frame. A ricrac trim has been tucked into a bias binding base trim.

TUTORIAL: MAKING A COVER ON THE BIAS

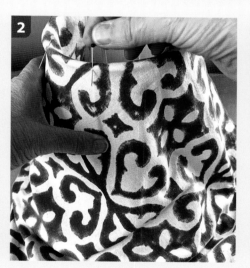

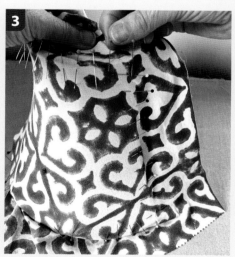

1 Hold the fabric – face down – at the bias or a 45-degree angle, and place the corner of this in the centre of the back of the lampshade frame; note the drawn arrow (indicating straight of grain) going at a 45-degree angle. Place pins in the top- and base ring corners where the bound opposite side struts meet the bound rings, that is, at the four corners.

2 Starting in one corner, working in a clockwise direction (or anti-clockwise, it is your choice), add pins where the struts meet the rings, including two or three down the bound side struts and around the base where the struts meet the bound base ring. You will probably need to re-position the original four pins in the 'corners'.

3 Now go round another circuit, this time – by pulling the handling allowance – stretching the fabric and adding more pins, including removing the pins already in place, stretching and re-pinning. Work around until you have a good taut cover but still some bounce (if pulled rigidly tight, the frame can be bent, which we do not want!). The pins should be around 1cm apart when completed.

Continued on the following page.

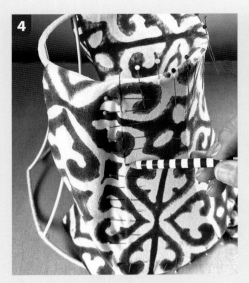

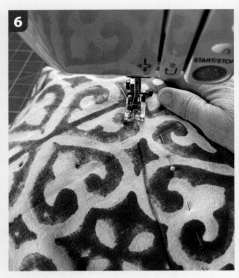

Once you are happy with the tension achieved on this first section, draw pencil (or chalk if using a dark fabric) lines down the middle of the two pinned side struts (only on top of the metal strut), and draw dots on the point where the struts meet the top and base rings. This is effectively making a pattern so it can be matched with another piece and re-positioned onto the frame.

Take the half cover off the frame, and lay it face down onto another piece of fabric, placed face up. Ensure the pre-drawn pencil/chalk arrows match up (*see* top left of image) – this means they have the grain line running in the same direction. You can try to pattern match the seam on one side by attaching pins down the drawn line and opening to check what will be at the seam; you can shift the fabric if you prefer to, but keep the arrows matching.

Attach the two pieces together with pins outside the drawn lines. Using matching colour thread, machine sew the seams exactly on the lines, starting 4cm before the drawn line and 4cm below it. Always machine the two seams in the same direction (top downwards). If using a thinner fabric, such as a lawn, machine the seam twice for strength. Then trim away the excess fabric from the sewn seams – around 3–4mm to the stitches.

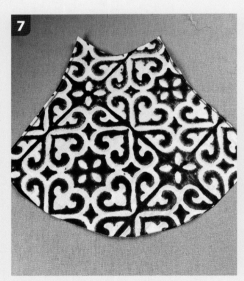

Add a smear of Pritt Stick on to the stitches if the fabric you have tends to fray. Now trim away the excess fabric from the top and base, cutting it in a curve to reflect the rings (this will open up the 'hole' at the top particularly) but keeping 4–5cm as the handling allowance. Put pins through the marked dots from one side to the other side, and place dots there too to complete the pattern.

Remove the tape from the two wrapped side struts. Now turn the cover inside out, and place it onto the frame, ensuring the seams are positioned in front of a side strut, which will be the one where you started/ended the tape binding. You will not need to open a seam, as it is small and will sit behind the strut. Pin in place, first around the top ring, matching your dots inside the cover to the struts/rings points. Turn it upside down and do the same around the base ring.

Next work around the frame pinning and pulling and pinning as you go, adding more pins with each circuit until you have them around 1cm apart and the cover is in the correct place with correct tension. It is important to keep the seams in front of the struts, so re-pin if necessary.

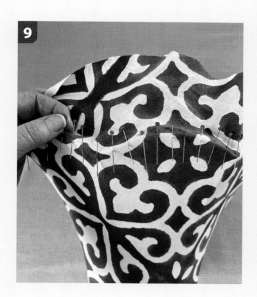

Using streetly stitch, sew the cover onto the top ring (start at a seam), taking out the pins as you go. Ensure the stitches are on the front of the ring. Use needle grabbers or grippers to aid getting the needle through into the bound taped rings. Now sew around the base ring. Your lampshade is ready to be completed without a lining, or to add a lining, *see* the relevant tutorials later in this chapter for your choice.

Making the Cover on the Straight

It is possible to work with the fabric on the straight of grain, although a perfect fit is needed, as it is not as forgiving as working with a bias cut. Consequently this is a little more challenging. The key benefit is that a defined pattern will be seen in the correct position.

Getting Started

Follow the same first three steps in 'Getting started – first steps' on page 98 as for making the cover on the bias.

Then cut your fabric into two pieces of the same size, taking into account where you wish the design to be placed:

- width of fabric – half of the circumference of the base ring
- height of fabric – that of the frame height
- add an extra 5cm all around these measurements for the handling allowance.

Follow the tutorial overleaf

The completed tailored lampshade made using the fabric on the straight of grain, meaning the pattern is positioned as printed.

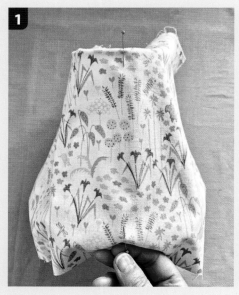

Place the cut fabric on half of the frame (face down), with the fabric positioned on the straight. Ensure there is 5cm spare all around the frame. Attach the fabric with one pin in the middle of the top ring, and one in the middle of the base ring. Ensure the fabric is not too tight and is able to sit on the shape of the bowed downward strut.

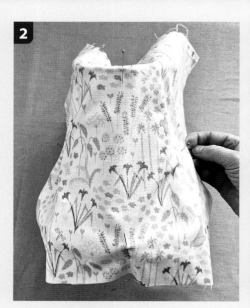

Now attach the fabric to the middle of each of the opposite bound side struts again with one pin each side. Check the fabric is exactly straight on the grain lines, vertically (the warp) and horizontally (the weft).

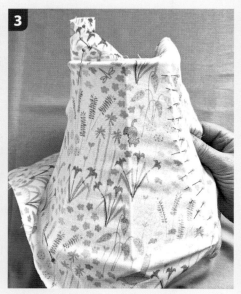

Next add pins from these mid-side points upwards – first place one on the side strut on the left, then place the next on the side strut on the right, that is, taking it in turns pinning up the struts, stretching it a little as you go. Repeat until you get to the top and then repeat downwards from the midpoints to the base ring. The fabric may look a bit loose at this stage.

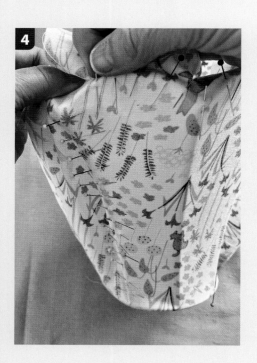

Now tighten the fabric vertically – add pins where the struts meet the top ring, and then again on the base ring. This should get rid of any wrinkles in the fabric on the weft (across the fabric). If the fabric has bowed away from the shape of the frame, re-pin horizontally until it hugs the struts.

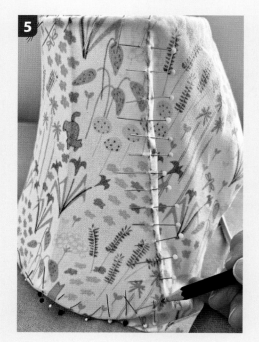

Pull all the fabric all around and pin until taut, ensuring that the straight of grain of the fabric is truly vertical in the middle of the half frame. Place pencil marks down the side struts as in step 4 of the bias made lampshade tutorial (although you won't have drawn arrows on this fabric) and continue from there with the same method.

TO LINE OR NOT TO LINE?

You may now wish to line the lampshade with a balloon lining you have already made or choose not to line it (*see* 'Choosing Whether to Line or Not Line Your Lampshade' in Chapter 4 for pros and cons). If the latter, you have a choice of how to complete the lampshade.

Completing an Unlined Lampshade

To make a lampshade without a lining, there are two things that you will want to hide:

- the stitching around the top and base rings
- the lampshade tape.

In order to do this, you can either use the 5cm excess fabric that you had as your handling allowance (this is suitable for lampshades made with the fabric on the bias only) or use bias binding.

PATTERN MATCHING ON STRETCHED LAMPSHADES

If you are using a fabric with a defined pattern, such as a stripe or check, it is important that the pattern is matched along the seams so that the stripe line, for example, meets its opposite partner on the second piece of fabric. It will look very messy otherwise, plus both pieces should follow the same fabric grain or weave line, and this will help with matching.

Make one half of the cover; then after marking it, take it off the frame and, when matching it to the second piece, put pins in the seam line and move it along until they match – then pin in place.

This can also work with some patterned fabrics, and although you may be able to match the pattern on one seam, you may not be able to control what appears on the second seam line. Just move the fabric onto the second piece, checking what the seams will look like, and make the best of it. With large patterns it is worth the effort. In all cases, remember to keep the grain line of the two pieces of fabric running in the same direction.

Take the time to ensure the pattern on striped and checked fabrics is matched at the seam.

How to Use the Handling Allowance as Your Trim

The handling allowance of 4–5cm is an approximate amount of fabric you will need to make this trim – each frame size needs a different amount, so use your scissors to trim it down if necessary. The method is based on tucking under the cut edge, and then folding it under and over to create a faux binding.

You can use the handling allowance remaining after making the lampshade to make a bias trim. This is suitable for larger lampshades and those made with the fabric on the bias.

1. Pull up the handling and turn under a few millimetres of the fabric, just to hide away the cut frayed edge.
2. Then take the fabric and bring it down in front of the ring, and below the stitches (to hide them). There should be enough fabric to go over the ring again after this stage.
3. Leaving the folded piece over the front stitches, take the remainder of it and fold it over the ring to the back.
4. Now pin it in place all the way around. Using slip stitch, sew it from front to back under the ring (*see* next tutorial for attaching bias binding for unlined lampshades).

This works best for larger lampshades. As the fabric is tight on smaller ones, use the following bias binding method.

How to Use Bias Binding as Your Trim on an Unlined Lampshade

Bias binding is a good trim to use because it is flexible and can easily be fashioned around the rings for the perfect fit, as opposed to a ribbon, which will not stretch. For lined lampshades, the bias is narrow, just covering the stitches made; with unlined lampshades, however, using a wider bias binding will hide both the stitches and the lampshade tape, which gives a much neater look.

In Chapter 8 you will learn how to make bias binding, so follow those instructions and then attach the bias as in this tutorial.

To add bias binding trims to an unlined lampshade, first carefully cut away all the excess fabric around the top and base rings to the stitches. Place a smear of Pritt Stick or other waxy glue to stop any fabric fraying – this will also help embed the stitches into the fabric and frame.

Using 18mm-wide bias binding, cut the lengths needed – the circumference of the rings plus 3cm (you can make or buy pre-made bias binding). Turn one end over by 5mm and attach it with a pin at the point where the seam is on the lampshade, ensuring it is positioned both over the front of the ring (hiding the stitches) and inside the ring (hiding the binding). It is best to pin as you go around, to keep it tight.

The binding will now be slip stitched onto the frame. Thread a needle with matching single thread (red used for contrast demonstration here) and put the needle through the top corner of the bias binding placed over the ring; then reposition the needle so it goes back under the ring to the front of the lampshade frame, just under the bias binding.

Then place the needle in the edge of the creased seam of the binding at the front, and slip the needle along inside it, around 1cm along. Come out again in the creased edge at the front. Then directly opposite where you have come out, take the needle back under the ring to the inside of the frame, and either slip stitch inside and along the inside crease of the bias, or just pick up a couple of threads of the bias, and come out into the front again.

Gently pull the end of the bias binding around the ring to fit, and place a pin in there; then repeat the sewing all the way around. This is better than pinning all of it in advance as it can become a bit baggy that way. At the end, trim the bias but leave 5mm; tuck this under so the two ends meet. Slip stitch down the seam. Repeat around the base using the same method if you wish, or add another trim to hide the stitches.

Completing a Lined Lampshade

Once you have made your lampshade, and trimmed away any excess fabric (*see* Step 1 below), you can now line it with the balloon lining you made earlier. The final steps will then be to add bindings or trimmings to complete the lined lampshade.

Inserting Your Balloon Lining into Your Tailored Lampshade

Follow these instructions to insert and sew your lining into place, as well as attaching gimbal covers to hide the necessary cutaways in the lining around them.

The stitches of your lining will be positioned on the front of the top and base rings, and various trims can be used to hide these. It is important that they can stretch to go around the curve of the rings, and so bias binding is ideal. The trim is not only to hide the stitching but also to add character and interest to your lampshade.

TUTORIAL: INSERTING A BALLOON LINING INTO A TAILORED LAMPSHADE INCLUDING GIMBAL COVERS

First, carefully cut away all the excess fabric around the top and base rings to the stitches, and run Pritt Stick around them. Take the lining and place your hand inside it, keeping the seams on the outside. Put the frame onto a table with the base uppermost and insert the lining into it, matching the lining seams with the seams of your outer cover. Pin it at the seam points on the base ring, attaching it to the sewn-in outer fabric and outside of the bound rings – put them with the sharps going upwards.

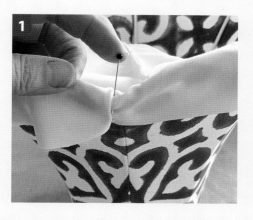

Place pins in the lining around the base, where the struts meet the base ring. This is where your dots or tailor's tacks should be positioned, and matching them exactly will help your lining be a good fit. Add a couple more between the struts; at this stage it is simply positioned.

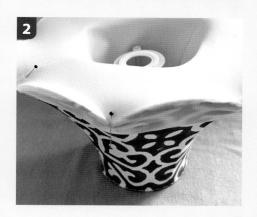

Now pull the lining inside through to the top of the frame, going around the light fitting up to the top. Attach it with pins at the seams first, and then match the dots on the lining fabric to the relevant struts on the top ring. This will cause gathering around the gimbals.

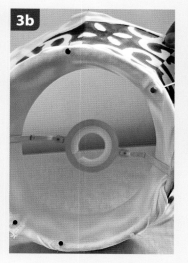

Using sharp scissors, cut the lining fabric so it fits around the gimbal – pull the fabric to one side, take hold of it, and snip from the top of the fabric down as far as you need it to go (every frame and lining are different). Be careful not to snip too much but just enough for the fabric to fit smoothly around the gimbal. Put pins in either side of it into the ring and repeat with the opposite one.

Continued on the following page.

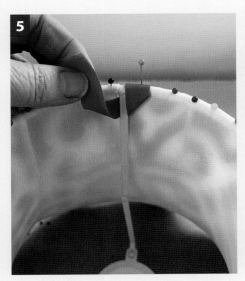

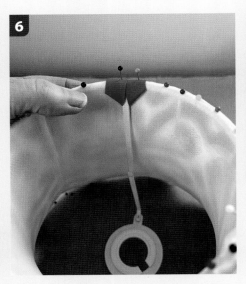

Make the gimbal covers (*see* Chapter 4) and place one so that it is positioned under the gimbal and either side of it, fabric-cut sides uppermost. Take one end in your hand, and bring it up and over the ring, so it becomes face up. Pin into the ring against the gimbal. Repeat with the other side of the gimbal cover, bringing it up and over the ring, the two sides just touching.

Pin both sides of the gimbal covers onto the ring, smoothing them out so they do not add bulk to the ring. They will be sewn into the cover along with the lining. Repeat for the other side. Add more pins all around the top ring, attaching the lining to the cover and tape, ensuring it is smooth all around.

Now sew the lining all around the top ring using streetly stitch, on the front of the ring. Hold the handling allowance of the lining to keep the tension, and take a pin out at a time to sew. Capture in the gimbal covers and make sure you are sewing through the main cover into the bound rings themselves.

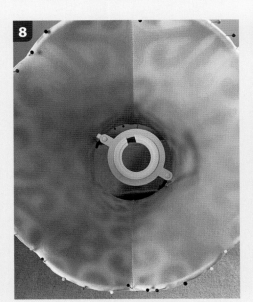

Now turn your attention to the lining around the base. Go around pulling and stretching the lining and pinning it in place until you are happy with its position. Look inside it and ensure it is a good, even, circular shape at the top, and that the seams sit exactly in front of the struts (so as not to be seen when lit). Pin all around and sew in place. You are now ready to make (as outlined in Chapter 8) and attach a bias binding trim.

Next, trim away the excess lining fabric and gimbal covers. A good tip is to pull the lining to a horizontal position or at 90 degrees to the lampshade, as this will avoid the scissors going into the fabric underneath. Pull it away and trim back to the stitches (be careful not to snip into them).

After snipping away the excess lining and gimbal covers, put some Pritt Stick onto the stitches. This will both embed the stitches but also prevent any fraying; if using Lycra, this should not be a problem, but it may be if you use linen, silks, or other fabrics. You are now ready to add the bias binding.

Adding Bias Binding to Complete Your Lined Lampshade

Decide which width of bias binding you would like to use – 12mm is ideal for smaller lampshades, and 15mm for larger. Cut and make enough bias binding to fit around the rings of your lampshade, plus 3cm extra (*see* Chapter 8 for making instructions). Slip stitch is used to attach the binding. Follow the tutorial.

TUTORIAL: ADDING BIAS BINDING TO COMPLETE YOUR LINED LAMPSHADE

Thread a curved or darner needle with matching thread to your cover (red is used here for demonstration purposes). With a pin, attach the folded-over end of the bias at the seam. Push the needle into the lining to the right of this, then into the corner of the folded bias. Now pick up a couple of threads of the lining exactly opposite where you have come out; then return to the folded edge of the bias, and slip the needle along inside the folded edge, around 1cm.

Pull the bias a little to fit, and add another pin a few centimetres along, attaching the bias to the ring, and carry on with slip stitch all the way around until you reach around 1cm from the end. It is best to only have a couple of pins in as you go, as you will need to stretch the bias to fit as you progress with the sewing.

When you reach around 1cm from the end, trim the bias binding so there is 5mm to fold underneath the end and abut it with the first piece. Pin it in place, and then continue slip stitching along and then down the seam. Add a couple of slip stitches, attaching the bias to the fabric underneath it at the front to secure it. Hopefully, the bias binding will be tight enough to stay in place, but if you think it needs it, add textile glue underneath it around the base and press firmly to set.

SECTIONAL LAMPSHADES

Sectional lampshades (also known as panelled lampshades) are made using regular traditional lampshade making methods and sewing skills; however, due to the shape of the frames, the covers are made in sections, as only two pieces of fabric simply cannot be tailored correctly. They are made either with the fabrics sewn directly onto the frame's bound struts, or sometimes made in separate sections and machined together, and then placed and sewn onto the frame.

Sectional Sewn-On Covers

For the tutorial, a curved bell tiffany frame is being used – it has a very small top ring with a much wider base ring in proportion, and it has highly curved struts connecting them. It is not possible to make the cover in two sections because it would not fit properly – the fabric should hug the curve of the struts so that the shape of the frame is visible. The solution is to make the cover in multiple sections. In this case there are eight struts and the cover is made in four sections, therefore each section covers two spaces. Measure this area, and cut the fabric pieces on the bias to fit, plus a handling allowance. The fabric being used has a small print, so there is no concern about pattern matching, but bear this is mind with larger patterns with sectional lampshades – you can use trims to separate them or try to match the seams.

Getting Started

To help achieve the best results:

- When binding the struts, because the tape will be left on permanently, you must have a few stitches in the flat knots at the base ring end, and the tail end trimmed neatly to the ring.
- The tutorial lampshade is made with a two-section Lycra balloon lining, but some shaped frames with extreme curves may benefit from having a lining placed on the outside of the frame instead (an external lining). If this is the case, it is worth binding every strut, so that when you look up inside the frame, every strut looks the same (instead of every other one, for example).
- It is important to sew each section on separately and then trim away the excess fabric so that the correct tension and fit is achieved.
- To help the fabric sit on the curves, stretch and pin the fabric up and down the sides first, and then along the top and base (rather like the method for making covers on the straight).
- When adding trims to the sewn strut seams, if your frame has outward curves only, they can be attached with a few stitches at the base of the strut, pulled up, and attached with a few more at the top; gluing or sewing will be needed all the way up with a non-stretch trim. The frame in the tutorial has curves inwards and outwards so it is better being glued all the way along.

Follow the tutorial to make a sectional lampshade.

Fringed tiffany lampshade by Sarah O'Dea of Shady and the Lamp, who used sectional techniques to make this beautiful lampshade.

The completed sectional lampshade using Liberty fabric, with hand sewn sections sewn directly onto the frame, and the sewn seams covered with bias binding.

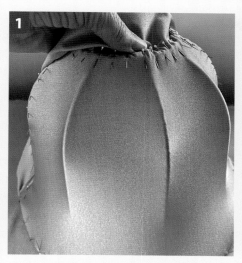

1 There are eight struts, and there will be four individual sections of fabric, therefore bind every other strut with tape, with the excess trimmed away. If a balloon lining is being fitted, using a stretch fabric is easier to work with than non-stretch (even positioned on the bias) because it has to fit into a really small top ring. Use lots of pins to position it correctly.

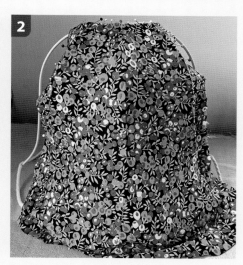

2 Now pin in place the first piece of fabric across the first section – the space between two struts – on the bias, right side/face up. To get a good fit, it is best to pin down and up the side struts to help the fabric hug the shape of the bowed struts – then pin in the top and base, sharing the stretch of the fabric evenly until it fits snugly all around.

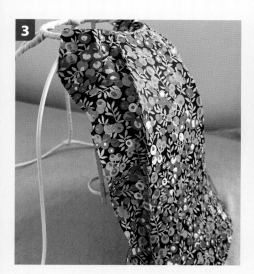

3 Hand sew this section of the cover in place using small, neat streetly stitches. Use the handling allowance to keep the tension and go all the way around this section, including the top and base rings. Place the stitches in the middle of the struts, as you will be adding another piece to the same strut.

4 Next, using small sharp scissors, trim away very carefully the excess fabric to the stitches, all the way around the first section. Add waxy glue to stop fraying and let it dry before starting the next section. When you add the next piece of fabric, use the handling allowance and place the pins on top of the stitches sewn in the first section, tailoring it to fit as you go round.

5 After you have added all four sections, trimmed away the excess fabric, and added waxy glue, place the lining inside the frame, being careful to pull it over the top and pinning in place. If you find it is a little wide inside, take it out and re-sew the seams on the machine if needed. Hand sew the lining in place all around and then trim away the excess fabric.

Continued on the following page.

Choose a trim to hide the stitches on the sewn struts – either the outer fabric bias binding or in a coordinating/contrast colour (here we have both) or a braid; if it has some stretch it can hug the curves of the frame. As these struts go inwards, gluing it in position is easier than sewing it along the edges of the trim. After the sewn seams are covered, the top and base rings are trimmed, and the lampshade completed.

Other frames that will need sectional sewn-on covers are square, rectangular, or frames that have cut corners. They can be made using four sections of fabric on the outside and again hand sewn into the bound struts. Ensure a perfect fit for these by using the fabric on the bias. Shield or half frames also have their fabric attached to the frame, which is bound with tape all the way around, and then sewn into.

Sewn onto the Frame Covers

There are times when making a cover for a frame, although it is being made in two pieces, will benefit from being fitted and sewn directly and permanently onto the bound opposite side struts – for example a bowed drum frame, which has a tiny waist but larger top and base rings. Using the usual stretched cover method would not work; this is because the waist is smaller than the rings and conse- quently the cover would not fit back on. Therefore the fabric needs to be positioned face up, stretched and pinned into position onto half of the bound frame, hand sewn onto the strut, excess fabric trimmed away, and then repeated on the other side. The stitches are then covered in bias binding strips or another trim of choice. A pre-made balloon lining

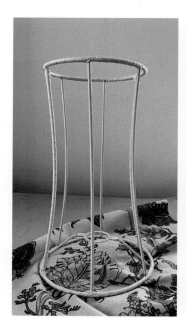

Sewn onto the frame covers: for some frames, such as this tall bowed drum, the stretched fabric needs to be positioned face up and then permanently sewn onto the bound side struts.

This is because if the cover pieces are sewn together off the frame, it will not be possible to re-position the cover over the rings as the frame has a narrow 'waist'. The sewn seams are covered in a trim.

This lampshade was made from two pieces of Union Jack fabric, which could not be pattern matched and so was messy at the seam. Therefore it has been sewn onto the side struts and the stitching covered with bias binding trim.

or external lining is attached, and trims sewn around the top and base rings.

As well as bowed drums, there may be other times when lampshades benefit from being directly sewn onto the frame. For example, having a bias binding covered seam edge may actually benefit the design – perhaps because the pattern match at the seam clashes or is messy, such as the Union Jack lampshade in the image here.

One other style of lampshade that has its side seams sewn onto the frame is the ruched gathered lampshade – *see* Chapter 6 for how to make these.

Pre-Sewn Sectional Covers

Pre-sewn sectional covers are not sewn onto bound struts of the frame, but are made in sections and sewn together on a sewing machine, and then fitted onto the frame. They often have different fabric designs so that multiple fabrics can be used for decorative effect. The frame is bound on every other strut (or every one, depending on how many panels you wish to have) – for example with a frame with eight spaces, you may decide to have four different fabric designs, each fitted across two struts, or eight different ones. One piece of fabric is then stretched and pinned across one section, and positioned face down, then a pencil/chalk mark is drawn on the fabric down the middle of both of the two struts. The fabric is then removed, and used as a template to place on top of another choice of fabric.

This works if each piece of fabric has roughly the same weight. However, if you are using, for example, lawn cotton on one section and wool fabric across the next, it is worth pinning each one on the frame in turn to achieve a perfect fit. The fabrics are then machine sewn together down the seams (and beyond for the handling allowance), attaching each one to the next and so on. Finally, the seams are trimmed away and waxy glue applied to stop fraying. The cover is then turned inside out and attached to the frame – as per the tuition for making a traditional hand sewn lampshade described earlier. The key thing is to ensure that the seams are each positioned perfectly behind the struts. You can choose to line it or not. *See* tutorials for completing hand sewn lampshades.

This standard sectional lampshade has different fabrics fashioned on the frame, which are then machine sewn together in advance of being placed onto and hand sewn on the frame.

LININGS FOR SECTIONAL LAMPSHADES

There are different approaches for the linings needed, dependent on the frame being used. The bell tiffany frame here has a balloon lining made in advance of the outside being sewn onto it. It is made in two sections (as per the 'How to Make a Balloon Lining' tutorial in Chapter 4) and then fitted inside the frame, hiding the struts. However, some frames may need more sections – rectangular frames, for example. In this case the lining is made in four sections:

1. Make and fit the lining in advance of the outer cover.
2. Pin the lining fabric (right side up) in four pieces on the outside of the frame, and when happy with the tension, mark the fabric with pencil/chalk down and alongside the struts on the inside of the cover.
3. Take the sections off the frame, and machine the seams together.
4. Re-fit the lining inside, then hand sew in place.

Other lampshades benefit from having the lining attached to the outside of the frame. This does not hide the metal or bound struts inside but does add depth to the fabric itself when lit. Experiment with the frames you have to see how many sections and which approach you may need.

CHAPTER 6

GATHERED AND PLEATED LAMPSHADES

Gathered and pleated lampshades have become a popular interiors item to have in all spaces, from living rooms to bedrooms and even bathrooms. One of the reasons for the rise in popularity is the increase in availability of hand block printed fabrics, as these are produced on thin linens and cottons. These are ideal for gathering, and look stunning when lit. You can make them full or sparsely gathered and have different coloured linings – either balloon or gathered or pleated too. Pleated lampshades, either knife or box pleated, can look better using silks or pure linens and cottons as they need to be pleated with crisp edges. Often the gathers or pleats speak for themselves but you can also add trims either along the base or tucked into the bias edgings.

Straight sided frames are the best to use, as the gathers or pleats need to be straight and taut, and run alongside the struts (the generic sizes available are listed in Chapter 4). You can also make lampshades that have mixed treatments – perhaps knife pleated at the base and gathered at the top or the reverse. This offers both the relaxed gather and the more formal pleat design, and they are a lovely pairing. For both styles, the fabric quantity needed is worked out in advance. This planning is essential – the fabric quantity needs to be shared out equally around the rings so that the gathers are the same fullness all the way around, the pleats are all the same size, and they sit nicely around the frame.

This gathered gingham lampshade has a double frilled trim added around the base ring to enhance the design. Lampshade by Jane Warren.

MAKING GATHERED LAMPSHADES

Preparation

There are factors to consider regarding the frame you are using and the fabric you wish to use, before you start making the lampshade.

- Work out the circumference of the lampshade base ring. For example a 10in/25.5cm base ring will have a circumference of 80.07cm (25.5cm × pi 3.14); round it down to 80cm.
- Then decide on the fullness of gathers you would like – perhaps × 1.5 if you would like to see more of the fabric pattern, or × 2 or even × 2.5 for a fuller gather. Once decided, work out how much fabric you will need (*see* table overleaf) – much depends on the weight of the fabric choice too.
- The amount of fabric and fullness is always calculated from the base ring measurement so make a small sample

This block printed fabric has been both gathered and pleated onto a French drum frame. 'Ikkatha' lampshade by Jane Warren.

on the lampshade frame, working between two struts. The amount of fabric you have between two base ring struts will also need to fit between the same two struts on the top ring – which may be a much smaller space.

- Get together the tools and materials needed (as outlined in Chapter 4) as well as your chosen fabric.

Fabric Quantities

This table gives you the amount of fabric you will need to make a gathered lampshade using different fullnesses. The amount is always calculated from the circumference of the base ring. You can then divide the amount by the number of struts on the frame to see if it will fit in between the struts (please note you will also need to allow for a 1cm turning each end of the fabric).

FULLNESS CALCULATIONS

Frame size		Fullness			
Base diameter	Circumference	× 1.5	× 2	× 2.5	× 3
8in/20.5cm	64.5cm	97cm	129cm	161cm	193.5cm
10in/25.5cm	80cm	120cm	160cm	200cm	240cm
12in/30.5cm	96cm	144cm	192cm	240cm	288cm
14in/35.5cm	111.5cm	167cm	223cm	279cm	334.5cm
16in/40.5cm	127cm	190.5cm	254cm	317.5cm	381cm
18in/45.5cm	143cm	214.5cm	286cm	357.5cm	429cm
20in/50.5cm	158.5cm	238cm	317cm	396cm	475.5cm

Notes: The figures have been rounded up or down for simplicity.

For fuller gathers and larger frames, the fabric will not be printed as wide as you need, so work with multiple widths of the fabric – see 'Using Widths of Fabric'.

To calculate the height of fabric required, measure the height of the frame and add 3cm working allowance both top and base, for example:
24cm + 6cm = 30cm high.

Add in a 1cm turning for each end of each length of fabric used.

Make small samples between two struts before you decide on fullness.

You do not have to be completely prescriptive about the amount of fabric to be used. If, for example, your frame has a 80cm circumference and six struts, and you have a piece of fabric that is 145cm wide, you can simply divide it by six and use that amount – but always share it equally around the frame, and leave 1cm each end for turnings.

Fabric Choice

With all the detail on fullness, the choice of fabric is paramount to a good gathered lampshade outcome. Using linens may seem a lovely choice – a natural fabric for a relaxed gathered look seems to go together; however, linens can be reasonably weighty and therefore do not gather well – they tend to bunch up. Far better are finer fabrics, such as silks, cottons, cotton mixes, and very fine linens, even muslin. Again it is a good idea to gather samples of fabric in preparation.

Using Widths of Fabric

With reference to the fabric quantity table, the amount needed may far exceed the regular width of fabric. Furnishing fabrics are often 137cm wide, and quilting or block printed fabrics are only 110–120cm wide. This will mean that widths of fabric will be needed to achieve the amount required for your frame. In these cases, you do not need to join the widths; indeed, machining them will only add bulk. Each piece will have a small 1cm turn under, hiding any raw edges, and it is always advisable to make the cover in two equal pieces for symmetry (or three or more if a really large frame).

For example, you may have the following specifications:

- frame size (base measurement): 12in/30.5cm diameter, 96cm circumference
- width of fabric: 110cm, patterned
- gather choice: × 2.

In this scenario, the fabric requirement will therefore be 192cm (that is, 2 × the circumference). You would cut two widths of fabric of 96cm plus 1cm turn at each end, so 98cm in length. You would need to ensure that each piece of fabric follows the same pattern – that is, it is pattern matched across the widths.

Positioning the Fabric Design

The tutorial lampshade will have bias binding attached to the top and base rings to both hide the stitches and complete the look. This is usually positioned around 1cm deep – therefore plan and place your fabric design, taking a note of this.

Plan the fabric design placement in advance, remembering that there will be a 1cm bias binding around the top and base rings. This fabric pattern is being positioned symmetrically.

The completed gathered lampshade after following the tutorial on page 117. You can either add bias binding or a gathered trim (*see* Chapter 8 for tuition).

Getting Started

For the tutorial, the frame used is an empire with:

- six struts
- a base diameter of 10in/25.5cm
- a base ring circumference of 80cm (diameter × pi)
- a base ring strut gap size of 13.3cm (circumference divided by 6)
- a top ring circumference of 41cm
- a top ring strut gap size of 6.9cm (circumference divided by 6).

The gather is × 1.5 fullness:

- The base ring circumference (80cm) × 1.5 means 120cm of fabric is needed. This divided by the 6 struts = 20cm; this amount needs to fit across the strut gap.
- The width of the cut fabric will be 120cm plus 1cm each end = 122cm.

- The height of the cut fabric will be that of frame (18cm) plus 3cm each top and base for handling allowance = 24cm.

First Steps

Once you have decided on the fullness of the gather:

1. Prepare the frame by tightly binding it with lampshade tape, top and base rings.
2. If you wish to pair the lampshade with a balloon lining, bind the two opposite side struts, make the lining, and put it to one side.
3. If you wish to have a gathered or pleated lining, then make this either in advance, on the frame, or after you have made this outer cover.

See Chapter 4 for tutorials on these steps.

Fabric Apportioning

To ensure that the fabric is shared out equally around the frame, it helps to make a diagram in advance with the measurements for clarity – these can then be transferred to the fabric.

1. Lay the ironed and cut fabric on a table, face up. Now place marks using a pencil or chalk along the top and base horizontal edges (within the 3cm handling allowance).
2. There will be a 1cm fold at each end. Therefore if the marks are every 20cm, the first one will be 21cm (as will the last). On the fabric, also draw a 3cm line in pencil/chalk up from the horizontal base edge. This line will be gathered and positioned on the base ring of the lampshade frame.

Transfer your workings onto the ironed fabric with pencil/chalk marks within the 3cm working allowance, remembering to allow for 1cm each end.

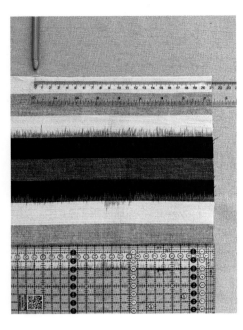

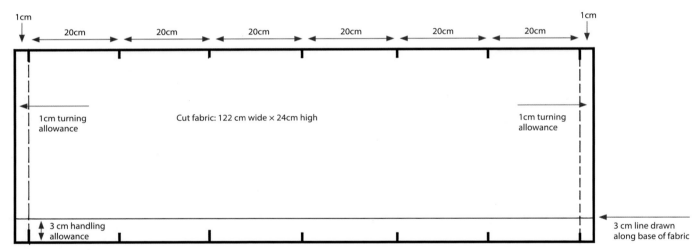

It helps to draw a plan of the fabric for a gathered lampshade, noting the strut gap fabric allowances; you can then transfer these marks onto the fabric. These measurements relate to the tutorial.

Gathering the Fabric

There are tutorials for gathering fabric in Chapter 4, so first decide which method you would like to use. In this tutorial, the fabric is gathered along the base using a sewing machine, and then gathered by hand around the top ring (*see* step 5 of tutorial). This gives you more control of the 'look' of your gathers, and is a better method if using thicker fabrics. Alternatively, you can pleat the fabric by hand around the top if you wish (*see* step 6 of tutorial).

Gather the prepared fabric along the base 3cm line, either on the sewing machine or by hand using a needle and running stitch. Then pull the loose threads left after the machining or by hand sewing, so that the length is gathered. Tweak it so that it fits around the base ring of the frame.

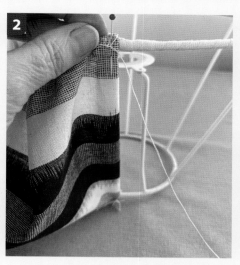

To attach the fabric, start by turning under 1cm at the end where the loose gathering threads are, and pin onto the front of the base ring; start where the binding started/ended. Also loosely pin in the other end to the top ring. Make sure the pins go under the threads of the gather, that is, they are free to still be pulled.

Pin the remainder of the fabric at the points where the pencil/chalk marks on the fabric match the struts, working around the ring. At the end, turn under the extra 1cm, and pin close to the first one. Pull the threads so that the gathers tighten all around until the fabric sits firmly on the ring. Pin the gathers in place, ensuring there are no flat parts of fabric.

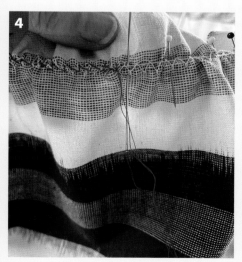

Next, using small streetly stitches (using either double thread or Terko or other thick single thread), hand sew the cover onto the front of the base ring, catching in the gathers as you go (sewn in red here for demonstration). You can sew over the gathering threads – there is no need to remove them as they will be hidden by the lining and bias trim at the end.

Pull the cover up to the top ring and, at the seam area, turn under and abut the two 1cm cut edges; pin in place. Match the pencil/chalk marks to the struts around the ring and pin. To gather the fabric on the frame, sew running stitch between the first and second strut. Pull the thread so that the fabric gathers – pull it up taut from the base, and pin in place the gathers. Wrapping the taut thread around the next pin helps keep the gathers in place. Alternatively, you can use running stitch around the complete top ring fabric, and then pull at the end to gather.

Continued on the following page.

Make sure the fabric gathers look straight between the top and base rings. Then hand sew the fabric around the top ring, using small streetly stitches to catch in the gathers, on the front of the ring. As an alternative, the fabric can be pleated: with your right hand, get hold of the fabric and push it under the fabric held by your left hand, then bring this over towards the right. Try to make the pleats all the same size. Pin and sew in place.

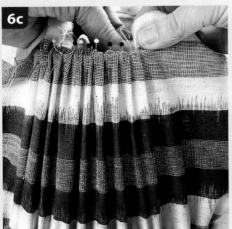

Sew all around the top ring, again ensuring the stitches are positioned on the front of the ring. Now carefully trim away the handling allowance to the stitches around both top and base rings; add waxy glue to stop fraying and embed the stitches. Snip away any frays. You can now add your lining and bias binding and trims to complete the lampshade.

Lining Your Gathered Lampshade

You may have pre-lined the frame with a balloon lining or a full gathered/pleated lining (*see* Chapter 4), or you can now add a pre-made balloon lining. In this tutorial, a semi-pleated lining will be fitted after the outer cover has been put in position. The choice is yours.

Semi-Gathered/Pleated Linings

As mentioned, the lampshade here will have a semi-pleated lining – the fabric will fit snugly around the base ring and will then be pleated around the smaller top ring.

To work out how much fabric is needed and how to apportion it:

1. Take the circumference of the base ring (80cm). This is the width of the fabric to work with, plus add on 1cm to each end, for the seam turn allowance. The height of the fabric is the frame (18cm) plus 3cm handling allowance top and base. Therefore cut amount is 82cm wide × 24cm high.

2. Divide the width amount (80cm) by the number of struts (6) = 13.33cm. This is the amount of fabric to fit between each strut. The fabric will be smooth around the base ring but still mark the fabric top and base to ensure accuracy.

3. Lay the cut lining fabric panel (face up) and mark the measurement points on the fabric (*see* the plan image for making the outer gathered cover).

4. Fold and turn under the 1cm widths at each end; ironing each one into a crisp fold helps maintain the fold.

You are now ready to make and attach the lining fabric to the lampshade by following the tutorial.

TUTORIAL: LINING A GATHERED LAMPSHADE

After making the strut marks on the lining and folding under the 1cm end pieces, place it right side down over the lampshade frame, and attach it 3cm up from the base edge, on the base ring. The 3cm is the handling allowance. Start at the key strut where all your workings are (that is, the binding tape knot and seams) and pin it in with the 1cm raw edge turned over towards you.

Then match the markings made on the lining with the struts, pin it around the base, again 3cm up from the lining edge. When you reach the end, you will have the extra 1cm fabric end; lay it over the first 1cm turning folded towards you. It should be a perfect fit around the ring. Sew the lining in place using streetly stitch on the front of the ring, ensuring the stitches go through into the tape. Snip away excess fabric to stitches.

Now pull the lining up inside the frame and then over the top ring to the front. Position the fabric with pins where your markings match the struts. Where there is a gimbal fitting, make a slit in the fabric using sharp scissors, just enough to allow the fabric to fit snugly around the gimbal. You will not have to make gimbal covers for this lining, as you can fold the cut edges under and then around it.

Pleat the fabric by eye/hand to fit between each strut – start at the seam as the fabric there will be facing in one direction and can be the first pleat. Make the pleats the same size all the way round. Alternatively you can gather the fabric – see overleaf. When in place, pin then hand sew all around on the front of the top ring, and trim away excess fabric to the stitches; add waxy glue. The lampshade is now ready to be trimmed.

You can also gather the lining instead of pleating it, by placing running stitches into the lining fabric in front of the top ring. Pull and gather, pin in place, and sew on the outside of the ring. Once the lining has been attached, the lampshade now needs the stitches to be hidden using trims (*see* Chapter 8).

Upside Gathered Covers

You may wish to have a lampshade with both a gathered cover and gathered lining, but only have a bias binding trim around one ring, for example the top ring. This is achieved by first putting in the lining, then attaching the outer cover upside down, and then pulling the fabric back on itself:

1. Plan the fabric, apportioning it and marking it with pencil/chalk accordingly.
2. Place the frame on the table, base ring upwards. Then position the fabric inside the frame, right side down, with the 3cm handling allowance flopping over the front of the ring.
3. Pin it in place, matching the pencil/chalk marks with each strut and the 1cm seam allowances on top of each other. Hand sew in place. Trim away excess fabric to the stitches.
4. Then bring the cover from the inside to the outside of the frame and pull it taut to the top. Pin it in place around the front of the top ring, matching the pencil/chalk marks with the struts.
5. Hand sew all around the top cover. Make sure all the stitches are on the front of the ring. Trim away the excess fabric to the stitches and cover them with waxy glue.
6. The top will need bias binding to hide the stitches; however, the base will have a lovely gathered effect with all stitches hidden inside.

To complete the gathered lampshade, bias binding has been added around the top ring and a frill trim has been added around the base (*see* Chapter 8 to make and attach these).

Upside gathered covers are positioned and sewn in place after an inner gathered or pleated lining is put inside the frame. They are made upside down so that after being sewn in place and turned right side up, there is no visible stitching at the base ring.

Gathered or Pleated Wide Tiffany Lampshades

These lampshades are made using wide tiffany frames, which are shallow in height and have a duplex fitting. They are often adorned with long silky fringes to add depth and design detail. The semi-gathered or semi-pleated approach is used here – that is, the fabric is snug around the base ring, and is then gathered or pleated at the small top ring. It helps to use a lightweight fabric, such as silks, satins, cottons, or voiles, so that the gathers or pleats can fit around the narrow top ring. It is not absolutely necessary to line them and if the lampshade is being positioned as a pendant, you may wish to see more of the outer fabric design, which a lining would hide. Therefore you can spray paint the metalware so that it becomes a feature or merges into the colour of the outer fabric. As with every hand sewn lampshade, make a sample first to see if it will benefit from being lined.

The wide tiffany lampshade in the tutorial is lined with a smooth satin-backed crêpe fabric, which is placed in position before the outer cover is fitted – this is beneficial for all pleated lampshades. It is possible to use the 'Upside Gathered Cover' method to make the outer cover, as demonstrated opposite; however you can also add the fabric face up in position, which is used in the tutorial to show the process.

Getting Started

The frame has a 'gallery' design around the base – this is where there are two parallel rings. In the tutorial, only the base ring has been bound with lampshade tape; however, if you wish to add trims around both of these rings, then bind both so that you can sew the trim in place. After binding, cut the correct amount of lining and outer cover fabric needed:

- The frame has a 41cm base diameter so the circumference is 129cm (rounded up); add 1cm each end, which gives a cut width of 131cm. The height of the frame (21cm) plus 6cm handling allowance gives a cut height of 27cm.
- Mark the top edge of both fabrics into eight (struts), so just over every 16cm.

Follow the tutorial overleaf to make this pleated wide tiffany lampshade. It has a Liberty silk fabric cover, a gathered lining in crepe-backed satin and is finished with a silky trim from Barnett Lawson, all hand sewn in place. Lampshade by Jane Warren.

Make the semi-gathered lining as per the previous tutorial; this time, however, it will be positioned into the frame first. Follow the tutorial to make this lampshade.

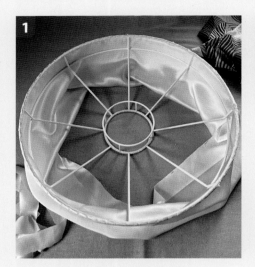

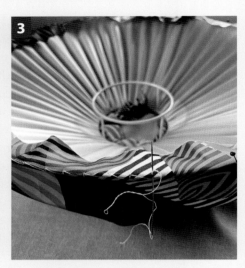

This lampshade has a semi-gathered lining (*see previous tutorial*). Starting at the bound seam, pin the lining fabric in place face down, with the 1cm seams turned over, keeping the 3cm working allowance free. Place pins all around – it should fit snugly, but not overly tight. Using streetly stitch, hand sew the lining in place on the front of the ring. Trim away the excess fabric, and add waxy glue to stop any fraying.

Turn the lining inside the frame, pull to the top, and pin it in place, matching the pencil/chalk marks with the struts. It is easier to position the pins inside the ring for this angled frame. Snip down into the lining below the gimbals, turn under these cut edges, pull up, and pin. Pull the lining over the front of the ring, and hand gather or pleat so that the fabric is as flat as possible.

Now trim away the excess lining fabric around the top of the stitches, and add waxy glue. Next, attach the outer cover, which is a semi-pleated one, right side up around the base ring, which will fit snugly, turning up the 1cm folded edges – position these on top of each other at the main binding strut. Pin it in place all around, and using streetly stitch sew around on the front of the ring.

Then pull the fabric up to the top ring, matching the pencil/chalk marks with the struts. Make some small pleats by eye – there will be quite a lot of fabric behind each one as the ratio of base to top ring is high, although pleats stay flatter than gathers. Pin them in place and sew through to the tape with small streetly stitches. Trim away excess and use waxy glue to stop any potential fraying.

Trim the base handling allowance to around 1–1.5 cm and fold it in front of the ring, positioning it under your choice of trim. This will ensure a neat interior when looking up into the lampshade. Adding a silky fringe around the base will add height – this one is 15cm long. Add a braid on top of the fringe (this is 12mm) as well as around the top ring. Sew these into place (using a curved needle helps) with small stitches in matching thread. Placing the frame on a lamp base aids the sewing.

Ruched Lampshades

Ruching is a gathered overlay of fabric that is pleated or gathered together to create a rippled effect. Ruched lampshades have their fabric ruched straight or diagonally across the frame and then permanently sewn into two opposite bound side struts – each side is made separately. The fabric is shaped by hand; there are no rules on size or form, they are simply fashioned into tucks across the frame.

First Steps

1. First, make a balloon lining and put it to one side.
2. Bind the frame around the top and base rings and both side struts (these will be permanently on the frame, so sew stitches into it and trim away the tail ends).
3. Then cut your fabric pieces the correct size: the frame in the tutorial has a base ring diameter of 15.5cm and is 15.5cm high; allow twice this amount for each side – therefore the cut fabric size is two squares of 31cm (this includes a handling allowance all around).
   Follow the tutorial steps to make the lampshade.

The completed ruched lampshade, which has a bias binding trim down the sides and top ring, and a handmade ruched ribbon trim around the base ring (*see* Chapter 8 for tuition).

TUTORIAL: MAKING A RUCHED LAMPSHADE

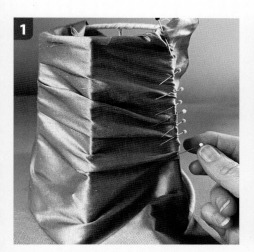

With the fabric on the straight, and allowing 5cm handling allowances all around, start pinning the fabric in one top corner of the frame and then down the side. Ruche the fabric as you go by making tucks in the fabric and pinning in place. Then work the other side, pulling the fabric across from the completed side, forming the pleats as you pin.

Once you are happy with the sides, now pin in at the top and base rings. Then, using small streetly stitches, hand sew down one side strut, around the base ring (on the front), up the opposite strut, and around the top ring (on the front of the ring). Trim away all the excess handling allowance closely to the stitches. Add waxy glue if the fabric frays.

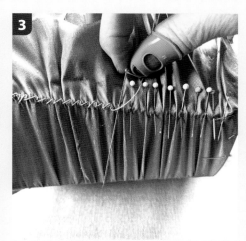

Repeat for the opposite side, pleating and pinning the fabric in place. Then sew – over the previous stitches – making the stitches as flat as possible. Insert the lining, bringing it over to the front and stitching in place. Make bias binding (12mm for this size) or use a braid trim, and attach it to the side struts to hide the stitches, either with small stitches or fabric glue, and around the top ring. You can either use bias around the base or add another trim, as per this lampshade.

PLEATED LAMPSHADES

The fabric used for pleated lampshades is made into crisp folds running vertically up the frame at regular intervals. The best frames to use are straight sided, as the pleats need the structure of the straight struts, the fabric being pulled up taut in front of them. Bear in mind that with a drum frame, the pleats will be the same size around the top and base rings, and so they are easier to make, whereas with empire or French drum frames, the pleats will need to fit within the smaller space between the struts on the top ring.

Linings for Pleated Lampshades

Making a balloon lining will give a soft light inside the lampshade, and these are often paired so there is no conflict between internal and external pleating. There is a choice as to when to fit the lining – either before making the outer pleated cover or afterwards. There are advantages to both:

- Fitting the lining *after* making the outer pleated cover will ensure that the tops of the pleats are captured in the smooth balloon lining, meaning there will be a flatter surface under the bias binding added at the end.
- If the lining is fitted inside the frame *before* making the outer cover, the outer pleats will not be pulled or over-handled and lose their form.

For the tutorial, the lampshade has a balloon lining fitted afterwards, but it is a personal choice (*see* Chapter 4 for lining information and tuition).

If you wish to have a pleated lining as well as an outer cover, then try to mimic the outer pleats in size – it may look very messy otherwise – and do position them first.

TYPES OF PLEATED LAMPSHADES

There are three main types of pleated lampshade: knife pleated, gap or spaced pleated, and box pleated. All need to be made with precision, both in the calculations working out their size and also by meticulously making the pleats so they do not curve or twist. They are therefore a more advanced technique but are a wonderful lampshade skill to learn. You can have fun in pleating to pattern, experimenting with the size of pleats, and creating a truly professional finish.

From top to bottom: samples of box pleats, spaced or gap pleats, and knife pleats.

Fabrics to Use for Pleats

Fabric with structure is best used for pleating, such as dupion silks and crisper linens and cottons, as the results will be sharp pleats that hold their shape, providing the grain line of the fabric is exactly followed. Some fabrics work better by being railroaded, as the weft threads may result in sharper pleats. Try samples before cutting your fabric, either ironing or using your fingernails to crease the pleats and then holding the sample in front of a lit bulb to see the final effect. It is also a good idea to leave your pinned sample pleats in place overnight to see if they hold their shape.

Perfect knife pleats made by Jennifer Fraser Lampshades for this beautiful pendant lampshade.

Making Knife Pleated Lampshades

Knife pleats are 'touching' or 'full' pleats and are formed by folding the fabric back on itself – that is, a pleat has three layers that are exactly the same size and therefore three times the amount of fabric is required for each one (for example 1cm pleats will each need 3cm of fabric). When the lampshade is lit, there should be no visible gaps between them – the pleats should abut each other. For smaller frames, narrow 1cm pleats can look very smart, whereas with larger frames, pleats of 2cm, 3cm or 4cm may work best – but this is wholly dependent on the dimensions of the base ring of the frame; the pleats must all be the same size and fit exactly around the ring. It is a good idea to try samples before committing to the decision. Although precision is vital as the fabric is folded to create the pleats, add a contingency amount to the cut length.

The completed knife pleated lampshade: each pleat is exactly the same size and they abut each other with no gaps. The lampshade has a gold Lycra balloon lining adding warmth, and a velvet stretch trim.

Working out the Maths

Pleat calculations are always worked out on the base ring circumference. We work them out to fit exactly between the strut gaps, this ensures the edge of the pleat runs alongside the metal strut edge. For the tutorial, the frame is a small French drum and it will have 1cm knife pleats:

- top ring 6in/15.5cm (circumference 48.67cm)
- base ring 8in/20.5cm (circumference 64.37cm)
- gap between base ring struts (6) 10.72cm, rounded up to 11cm
- height 6in/15.5cm.

1. The pleats will be 1cm wide around the base ring, and the gap between struts 11cm, therefore there will be 11 pleats between the struts. They will be tweaked so they are a bit smaller to fit in equally around the circumference (64.37cm not a true 66cm).
2. For the width, you need three times the fabric to make the 1cm pleats, therefore 11cm × 3 = 33cm (between each strut) × 6 struts = 198cm, plus 1cm for each cut length, plus 5cm contingency to handle (205cm). As this amount is greater than one width of fabric, it will need to be cut into two equal strips: two sections of 106cm (99cm for pleats, 2cm for end turnings, 5cm for contingency). If using a patterned fabric, take the repeat into consideration. For larger frames, cut more strips. Note that the first fold will always be the width size of the chosen pleat size.
3. The height will be 15.5cm plus working allowance = 22cm. Cut the strips of fabric absolutely square and straight, to help form accurate pleats.

The Process

The fabric will be pleated and made on the frame, forming crisp pleats, and pinned in place working around the frame. You can iron the pleats in advance; however, they may not fit exactly or may change width as they are ironed, so try a sample in advance to see if that works – every fabric responds differently to pleating. In the tutorial, the lampshade is pleated as it is being made, which offers greater accuracy for each knife pleat and the fit. You can make the lampshade with the frame standing up on the table, but with smaller or mid-size frames it may be easier to make it on its side on your knees (look out for pins catching at your clothes – a tray may be useful).

Getting Started

1. Get together the tools and materials needed (as outlined in Chapter 4) as well as your chosen fabric.
2. Lay the pressed strip of fabric face up on a table and, with pencil/chalk, draw a 3cm horizontal line up from the base. This indicates where the fabric will be attached to the base ring and will help ensure your fabric is straight when pleating. Use a set square to aid precision.
3. Now within the working allowance, make pencil/chalk marks to indicate the pleat allowance – in this case, every 3cm along base and top. Do not forget that the first 1cm will be turned under, so allow a 4cm mark at the start.
4. You can also make small marks on the bound rings with 1cm marks (the pleat size) so that you know where each pleat is to be placed.

5. When you start making the pleats, make them as crisp as possible as you pleat, ensuring you follow the grain of the fabric, to get the best effect and for them to stay in place – use your fingernails to aid this.
6. Because this frame has a smaller top ring than base ring, although each pleat will be creased vertically at 3cm, the extra fabric will be tucked underneath to create smaller top pleats; you will see visually where they should lie as you pleat because each one needs to be vertical and at a right angle to the ring.

First Steps

Bind the frame with lampshade tape. Make a balloon lining and put it to one side to fit later, or fit it in place first. Remove the side binding tapes. If you wish to have a gathered or pleated lining, make these on the frame in advance of the outer cover.

Now follow the tutorial steps.

TUTORIAL: MAKING A KNIFE PLEATED LAMPSHADE

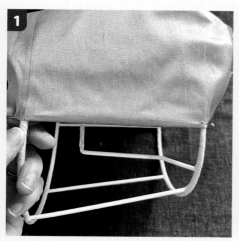

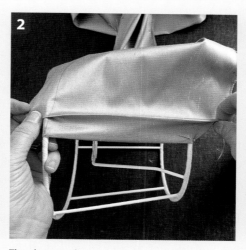

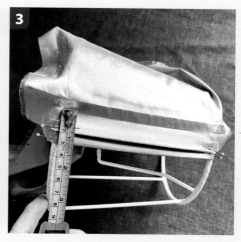

With the fabric face up, fold under 1cm, which forms the first pleat, and attach it with a pin to the base of the bound lampshade frame on your horizontal pencil/chalk line, at the working strut (the one where your binding started/ended). Pull up the fabric and pin it into the top ring, ensuring the fold follows the grain of the fabric. Make a crisp pleat as you pull up.

The pleats on the completed lampshade will go in a left-to-right direction. Lay the frame on its side (base side on your left) and find the first pencil/chalk mark you made both top and base of the fabric. Take hold of the handling allowance and, using your fingers/nails, make a sharp fold or pleat so that they connect at those marked points, ensuring you are following the grain line of the fabric.

Now bring the pleat over towards the start of the fabric and, using a tape measure to ensure that there is exactly 1cm at the base, pin this pleat in place on the base ring. Take it to the top ring, and pin that in place too. There will not be 1cm intervals at the top as there is less room between the struts, so the same amount of fabric will need to be fitted in to a smaller pleat – all the top pleats should be placed directly vertically up from the base.

Continued on the following page.

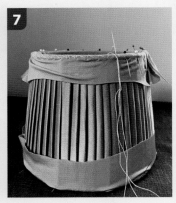

Keep pleating until you reach the first strut, measuring each pleat and slightly tweaking if necessary so that they fit in (in this case, ensuring eleven exactly fit between the struts). I tend to make three pleats at the base, and then turn the frame the other way and connect the three at the top, but you can do one at a time if preferred. Keep checking the size and that the pleats abut each other. Hold the frame to a light to check there are no gaps.

If you have another piece of fabric to work with, trim away the end of the first piece until it is just over the strut. Now turn under the first 1cm of the second piece, and place it on top of the strut, pinning base and top – this is your first pleat of the fabric. You can stitch the pleats you have made so far; however, ensure the very first pleat is left unstitched so the fabric at the end can be tucked under it. Pull the handling allowance up tight and streetly stitch on the front of the ring.

After pinning the next piece of fabric all the way around – constantly checking the size and position of the pleats, streetly stitch it in place except for the last couple of pleats. Trim away the excess fabric, leaving 2cm at the end, and tuck this piece under the very first pleat you made. Pull tightly and pin in place both top and base. Streetly stitch these in place.

The lampshade is now ready to have the balloon lining fitted and trims added. This lampshade has a gold Lycra lining, which is hand sewn in place using streetly stitch. When you position the lining, take care not to manhandle the outer pleats, so as not to lose their shape slightly. Add your trim of choice.

Once you have made the lampshade following the tutorial, complete it by fitting the balloon lining (if being positioned afterwards) and the bias trims (instructions for fitting both are the same as for traditional lampshades, in Chapter 5).

Making Spaced or Gap Pleated Lampshades

These pleats touch accurately on the front of the lampshade, but have a gap at the back of them, so they are not full and consequently use less fabric – that is, they are not made with the 3 to 1 ratio used for knife pleats. For example, a 2cm pleat may be made with 4.5cm of fabric rather than 6cm of fabric. The advantages of this type of pleat are:

- You can use slightly thicker fabrics, as there is less bulk than with full pleats.
- It is more cost effective, using less fabric meterage.
- You can choose to have a pleated base and a gathered top, as there is less fabric to fit around a smaller top ring, for a more relaxed look.

Working out the Maths

The pleats need to be worked out size-wise so that a number of equal-size pleats fit between the struts, and therefore the base ring. There is a formula to follow for spaced pleats, which is:

- The gap between struts divided by the required pleat size = the number of pleats.
- The gap between struts multiplied by the fabric fullness required, divided by the number of pleats = the amount of fabric to be used for each pleat.
- This amount can be marked onto the fabric, and then shaped into smaller pleat sizes.

You may find that you need to tweak the pleat size so you have a round number to fit between the struts (*see* the example below when calculating the measurements for the tutorial).

For the tutorial, the lampshade is gap pleated around the base, and gathered around the top ring; however, you can pleat around the top ring if preferred. The frame used is a 12in/30.5cm (metric rounded up to 31cm) French drum with the following dimensions and fabric/pleat requirements:

- base ring = 12in/31cm, so circumference = 97.34cm, rounded down to 97cm
- top ring = 8in/20.5cm
- slope height = 8in/20.5cm
- 6 struts
- duplex fitting
- × 2 fullness of fabric to make 1.5cm wide pleats.

With a base ring circumference of 97cm, and 6 struts, the gap between each strut is 16.17cm, which is rounded down to 16cm. Therefore, using the formula above:

- The gap between struts (16cm) divided by the required pleat size (1.5cm) = 10.66 (number of pleats). However, we need the number of pleats between the struts (and the whole base ring) to be equal, so tweaking the outcome by having slightly larger pleats (1.6cm, as opposed to 1.5cm) gives:
  - Gap between struts (16cm) divided by pleat size (1.6cm) = 10.
  - This means we can have 10 × 1.6cm pleats between each strut. This means we are allowing a 96cm, as opposed to a 97cm, circumference, so slightly tweak the pleats by a millimetre for total accuracy.
- The gap between struts (16cm) × fullness (× 2) = 32cm, divided by the number of pleats (10) = 3.2cm. This gives the amount of fabric to make each pleat.
- 3.2cm will be made into 1.6cm pleats, so the cut fabric will be marked every 3.2cm, not forgetting the 1.6cm to start with to fold under.

Follow the tutorial on the next page to make the lampshade with spaced/gap pleats around the base ring and gathered fabric around the top ring.

The Process

Cut the amount of fabric needed to make the lampshade. There is × 2 fullness, so:

- Circumference (97cm) × 2 (amount of fullness) = 194cm.
- This is wider than the fabric width, so two equal lengths are required, each being 97cm, plus 1.6cm at each end for turning under. The lengths of fabric will not be joined in advance, but added as the lampshade is made.
- Therefore each piece is cut 100cm wide × 26cm high (20.5cm) frame height plus 3cm working allowance. Add more width for contingency if you wish. The two fabric pieces have also been cut to ensure pattern matching across the whole lampshade.

First Steps

Bind the frame with lampshade tape. Make a balloon lining and put it to one side to fit later, or fit it in place first – it is personal choice. Remove the side binding tapes. If you wish to have a gathered or pleated lining, make these on the frame in advance of the outer cover.

Once you have made the lampshade following the tutorial, complete it by fitting the balloon lining and the bias trims.

Follow the tutorial steps.

TUTORIAL: MAKING A SPACED OR GAP PLEATED LAMPSHADE

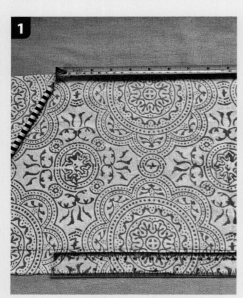

Cut two widths of fabric – ensure they pattern match. Draw a 3cm horizontal line up from the base. Fold under the first 1.6cm at the right hand end. Then draw pencil/chalk marks at every fabric pleat allowance, so every 3.2cm along the base of the fabric, within the 3cm handling allowance. Place pencil/chalk marks within the 3cm handling allowance where the fabric will be attached to the top ring struts – that is, every 32cm (33.6cm for the first one).

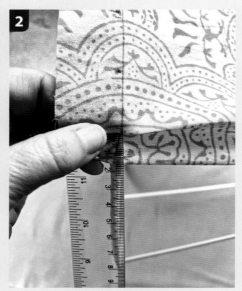

On the first piece of (ironed) fabric, fold under the 1.6cm edge. Pin at the 3cm line to the base ring and in the top ring over the working strut. Using a tape measure, and with the frame on its side or on the table, hold the fabric at the first pencil/chalk mark along and fold the fabric so that it makes the required pleat size (in this case, 1.6cm). Make the pleat crisp in the first few centimetres of fabric up the pleat and pin this pleat onto the base ring if you are having a gathered top. If having a pleated top, make the fabric crisp up to the top ring.

Now work around the ring to the first strut, measuring each pleat for accuracy (1.6cm), so that there is the right number of pleats in the strut gap (ten). If you have more or less, tweak each pleat until they fit correctly. Carry on around the frame until you get to the end of the first strip of fabric (that is, half the frame). Trim away any excess fabric, leaving 2cm over the strut. Join the next piece of fabric with the 1.6cm turned under and place it over the strut; it will be the next pleat.

Keep pleating and pinning around the base ring. At the end, snip away excess width fabric, apart from 2cm – place this piece over the strut (this will be the last pleat), and then using the second piece of fabric, pin the very first pleat next to this, in front of the strut. Check the pleats are the same size all the way around, and that there is the correct number of pleats in between the struts. Using streetly stitch, sew the cover onto the base ring on the front of the ring, capturing in the edges of each pleat.

Attach the cover to the top ring now – pull the cover up taut at the seam and pin into place. Then work around the top ring, matching the pencil/chalk marks to the struts. If you wish to pleat at the top, work your way around, pleating by eye and ensuring that the pleats are truly vertical. To have a gathered top – as here – use running stitch between the first two struts, gather and pin in place (*see* gathered lampshade making tutorial), then move on to the next strut and repeat.

When you reach the end, sew the cover onto the front of the top ring, holding onto and pulling the working allowance at all times to keep the taut lines of the pleats and/or gathers in place. When completed, trim away the excess handling allowance fabric around the top and base; place waxy glue around the stitches to both avoid fraying and to set in the stitches.

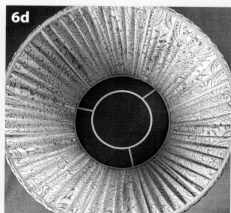

Pleated/Gathered Lampshades

On pleated/gathered lampshades, the base and top rings have different treatments to each other. For example, the fabric may be gathered around the base ring and pleated around the top (*see* step 6 of the gathered lampshade tuition). Alternatively, it may be the other way around – in the previous tutorial, the lampshade has a pleated base with a gathered top. You can mix and match and even pleat to pattern if possible.

Follow the tutorial to make this box pleated lampshade, which has a patterned balloon lining and the box pleats smocked together. Made by Jane Warren.

This pleated/gathered lampshade has had its fabric pleated to pattern around the top ring.

Making Box Pleated Lampshades

Box pleats are two knife pleats folded in different directions that meet behind a wide pleat in front (*see* image of pleat styles in the introduction). Straight sided frames are required, and using a drum frame will mean the pleats are the same size vertically. However, with an empire frame or French drum, you can make either:

- 'spaced' pleats, where they are close together around the top ring, and then kept the same size vertically but are spaced with gaps around the larger base ring
- 'touching' pleats, where the vertical pleats widen down the height to abut each other around the base.
Both methods are illustrated in the tutorial.

After they have been sewn onto the frame, the box pleats can then be made more complex by smocking them together, creating different patterns and shapes, and you can add beads or stitch colours too. This is particularly effective with touching pleat styles. As with knife pleats, box pleats use three times the amount of fabric to make each pleat, although it is possible to use less fabric and make your pleats not touching at the back. As with all pleated lampshades, the pleat sizes and fabric requirements are calculated, but because fabric takes up space when it is folded, you need to add a contingency to the length.

Working out the Maths

Unlike knife pleats, box pleating calculations are made using the top ring circumference. This is because the ring is smaller (unless you are using a true drum frame) and the pleats need to fit exactly. They can then either have gaps or be splayed out to fit around the base.

For the tutorial, the frame is a French drum with the following dimensions:

- top ring = 7in/18cm (circumference 56.52cm)
- gap between top ring struts (6) = 9.42cm rounded up to 9.5cm
- base ring = 10in/25.5cm (circumference 80cm)
- gap between base ring struts (6) = 13.33cm
- height = 7in/18cm.

We can use these figures to calculate the following:

- We want a pleat size of 2.5cm each around the top ring, and the gap between the struts is 9.5cm. However, when 9.5cm is divided by 2.5cm, the answer is 3.8 (number of pleats) but we need a whole number.
- Therefore tweak the pleat size a little to reach a round number. If each pleat is 2.4cm, this works out as a round number of 4 (9.5 divided by 2.4 = 3.96, rounded up to 4).
- Each pleat will therefore be 2.4cm wide, and there will be 4 pleats between each top ring strut space (so 4 × 6 struts = 24 in all).
- We use × 3 the amount of fabric, therefore each pleat will need 2.4cm × 3 = 7.2cm, so the amount of fabric for each strut space is 7.2cm × 4 (number of pleats) = 28.8cm; round it up to 29cm.
- There are six struts, therefore the whole width of fabric needed is 29cm × 6 = 174cm.
- Because 174cm is wider than one width of fabric, cut two equal pieces but ensure you add on 5cm contingency, plus 1.5cm to each end. Therefore each piece will be 87cm (half of 174cm) plus 5cm contingency and 3cm end turns = 95cm wide.
- The height of the frame is 18cm; add on 6cm handling allowance = 24cm cut height.

The Process

The fabric is pleated to size; it is helpful to do this on a table and to then iron the pleats in advance, as effectively you are making two opposite-facing knife pleats, behind a 'box' of fabric, which need to be crisp and follow the grain of the fabric.

1. Lay the pressed strip of fabric face up on a table and draw a horizontal line 3cm down from top. This is the working allowance and where the fabric will be attached to the top ring, which helps ensure accuracy.
2. Within the 3cm working allowance, place pencil/chalk marks along the fabric to mark the pleat points size; the first mark will be 1.5cm along, then every 2.4cm (the finished width of the pleats), then repeat along the base edge of the fabric, ensuring they line up with the top marks.
3. Decide if you wish to splay the pleats at the base when it is being attached to the frame, so that they touch, or leave the pleats the same size vertically and have a space or gap at the base – see tutorial for instruction.
4. You can also make small marks on the bound rings every 2.4cm (pleat size) so you know where each is to be placed.

First Steps

First, bind the frame and make a balloon lining. If you are using a stretch Lycra fabric, you can put it to one side and fit it afterwards; however, the lining in the tutorial has been made with non-stretch cotton fabric on the bias, and so it has been fitted in place before the pleated outer. If you wish to have a gathered or pleated lining, again make these on the frame in advance of the outer cover, but check with samples in advance as the pleats and gathers may clash or look messy when the lampshade is lit.

Follow the tutorial overleaf to make a box pleated lampshade.

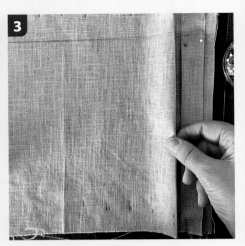

With the fabric laid on a table or ironing board, start pleating at the right-hand edge of fabric as follows. Connect the first two pencil/chalk marks, hold them together, and crease the left edge of fabric so that it folds behind (to the left) into a pleat. Press and pin it in place. Repeat at the base of the fabric. On the base, make sure the pins are placed near the cut edge of the fabric.

Then bring the next pencil/chalk mark on the left over to the following one on the left, again creasing the fabric where they join, folding it under to the right, and pinning in place. This makes the first box pleat at the front. Check the measurement is correct (2.4cm in this case), pin in place, and repeat at the base. Ensure the 3cm horizontal pencil line is connected – this helps keep the fabric on the straight of grain.

The next pleat will be made by bringing the next pencil/chalk mark on the left over to the right, abutting the first box pleat; fold the fabric under to the left. You can do the top and base pleats at the same time or one after the other. It helps to press them with your iron as you go for accuracy. Again, join the next dots, forming the box pleats; repeat at the base, measuring as you go along.

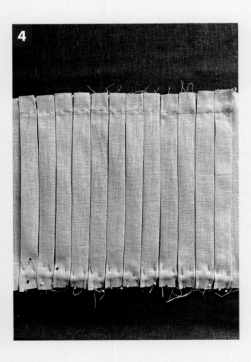

Work your way along the length of the fabric, pleating and pinning. Here we have twelve pleats that fit around half the frame. It helps to place running stitch along the top pleats to keep them straight and in place. Once complete, iron the fabric down the pleats, unless you are having touching pleats (see step 7), ensuring the pleats meet at the back as well as the front; tweak if necessary. Repeat for the second length of fabric.

Pin the fabric to the top ring of the frame at the first strut (where the seam of the lining is) on the 3cm line. Leave 1.5cm free at this point. Carry on pinning the pleats around the top ring, ensuring you have exactly four (in this example) fitting between each strut. Cut away excess fabric at the end, apart from 1.5cm. Add the second length of fabric, tucking the 1.5cm end under the previous pleat. Sew around the top. Now decide if you are having spaced or touching pleats around the base. or touching.

6

For spaced pleats, the gap between base ring struts = 13.33cm, and top ring struts = 9.50cm (in which our 4 pleats fit). The difference is 3.83cm. This divided by 4 (pleats) = 9.5mms, and half of this (that is, to find the gap either side) = 4.8mm. Place the frame with the base ring up, and pull out some of the fabric behind the pleats (which stay the same size), leaving 4.8mm either side. Alternatively, you can do this by eye. Pin around the base and hand sew in place on the front of the rings – unless you are smocking the pleats, which should be done first.

7

For touching pleats, iron them only at the top of the fabric, then simply pull each pleat at the base so that each one touches its neighbour. Make crisp folds by hand from the top, angling them downwards. Check to see that there is the same amount of fabric folded underneath by holding the frame up to the light. Then repeat, pinning around the frame. Hand sew in place on the front of the rings, unless you are smocking the pleats, which should be done first.

EMBELLISHING YOUR BOX PLEATS

Box pleats are decorative enough if making the spaced-pleated style, as the precision and straight edges look neat and orderly. However, these lampshades are often made using plain fabrics (that is because two thirds of the fabric design is hidden behind the main pleat), so in order to add more character, consider using a patterned lining (as in the example in the tutorial) and/or smocking. Before you start smocking, however, leave the sewing of the cover onto the base ring until you have completed it, otherwise the pleats will be too tight to work with.

1. Measure down from the top edge of the lampshade to where you wish to start the smocking, and mark these points accurately with tailor's tacks or pins and repeat around the lampshade. Then pinch the edges of these pleats, and sew them together either using a vibrant thread as part of the decoration or make small stitches using matching thread.
2. Then stitch the other sides of the already attached pleats to the next ones below them – this will form a smocking design; you can do as many and as often as you wish.
3. When you have completed the smocking, next hand sew the fabric around the base ring. Trim away the excess fabric, place waxy glue on the stitches, and then complete the lampshade by adding bias binding.

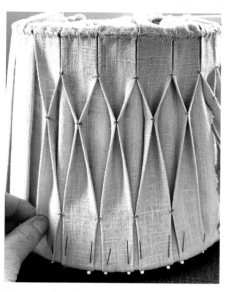

To ensure that the smocking points are sewn and measured accurately, sew tailor's tacks. You can choose where to smock and how often, but it is vital the smocking points are lined up.

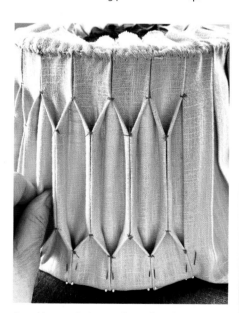

Smocking works best with touching box pleats (step 7 in tutorial), as there is less tension across the fabric. Coloured thread has been used here but you can also add beads to the sewn points.

Adding 'Mock' Box Pleats

While box pleats are made from a continuous piece of fabric, you can also add individual strips of fabric on top of a stretched lampshade cover – these are mock box pleats, also known as fake or faux pleats. The advantage is that you can mix your fabric designs for interest, and they take less time than true box pleating.

First bind your frame with lampshade tape; make a balloon lining if required. Then cover your frame with a tailored cover – on the bias for a perfect fit (*see* Chapter 5 for instruction). Then:

1. Decide on the widths of the pleats you wish to have – work it so that they fit equally around the rings. For example, if the top ring has a circumference of 54cm, and has six struts, you can have three pleats of 3cm between each set of struts.

2. Next make fabric tubes (*see* Chapter 8) with a finished size of 3cm. Pin them around the top ring and sew in place. If you are using a drum frame, the pleats will fit perfectly around both rings, but with a French drum or an empire they will be positioned apart at the base.

3. You can also cut smaller strips of fabric in a different colour and place them on to the larger box pleats, as in the image.

4. You can smock the pleats if required, and then hand sew around the base ring.

5. Add your balloon lining if applicable, and then a bias binding trim.

'Shadow Pleat Coolie' lampshade by Casey Ryan of Ryan Coombes Designs, who has worked with strips of two colours of silk and then attached them individually on top of the original box pleats.

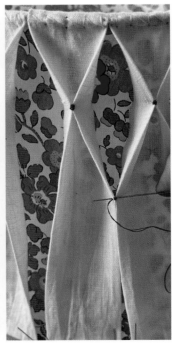

This frame has a stretched tailored cover in a Liberty fabric, with chalk-white linen mock pleats around it, which have been smocked to reveal the colour underneath.

OTHER GATHERED AND PLEATED LAMPSHADES: AN INTRODUCTION

Now that you have learnt the key techniques for making gathered and pleated lampshades, there are other traditional styles you can make using these skills. Here you will find an introduction to some of these and a guide as to how they are made. In all cases, take note of the best way to line, or interline, the lampshades, and plan your choice in advance.

- If using a really thin fabric, place a tailored interlining or undercover onto the front of the frame.
- It is beneficial to add a balloon lining to hide the metalware (and add depth to the light emitted), but if you decide not to, ensure the interlining is positioned with the seams facing upwards so they are not visible inside the frame.

Gathered Layered Lampshades

Lampshades can be made using a layering of thin or fine fabrics, such as chiffon, muslin, or georgette (a lightweight crêpe), to give interest with colour depths. The fabric is gathered and placed over a different coloured stretched tailored undercover or top interlining – when the lampshade is lit, a different colour is revealed. The tailored undercover or interlining hides the metal struts as the outer fabric is thin. To add further depth, a balloon lining can be fitted either in a warm colour or matching that of the outer cover. Use a straight sided or a slightly bowed empire frame; it is best to use the latter with a collar frame so that the gathers can be clinched in with a trim (*see* 'Kitchen Lampshades' in Chapter 7).

The Process

1. Bind the frame and make a balloon lining (if applicable).
2. Make a stretched tailored outer cover (*see* Chapter 5) on the bias and hand sew it onto the frame.
3. Decide the fullness of the gathers you wish to have on the outer fabric. Work out how much is needed to cut (usually 3 × the base ring circumference for these really thin fabrics) and how much is needed between each strut.
4. Gather it by hand on the frame using running stitch, pinning it around, sharing the gathers equally between the struts. Hand sew it onto the front of the rings. Trim away all excess fabric, add the balloon lining if applicable, and add your chosen trims to complete the lampshade.

This lampshade has a gathered chiffon outer cover being positioned on a gold silk tailored cover. The two colours will look warm and inviting when lit, and a balloon lining in cream will add depth too.

Swathed Pleated/Gathered Lampshades

Swathed lampshades have fabric either pleated or gathered diagonally across a frame and are made using bowed empire frames. Work out the maths beforehand when pleating – exact pleat sizes will need to be fitted in the strut gaps both top and base. Spaced or gap pleats may be a better approach unless using very fine fabrics. Experiment with fabrics – fine materials such as chiffon, very light cottons, muslin, or georgette work well. You can also use different colours of fabric in each strut section to showcase the pleats, resulting in lovely designs. A balloon lining is best for these lampshades for a smooth, uncluttered look.

First decide how many struts you wish your fabric to run across, for example by attaching the fabric on the base ring at a strut, then pulling it up to the top ring but across two struts to the right (you are swathing it up and across); alternatively you may wish the fabric to be swathed around half of the frame. Allow three times the amount of fabric for swathed lampshades, and decide on the pleat allowance (three times for touching knife pleats or less for spaced pleats).

This vintage lampshade has fine chiffon fabric swathed around the bowed oval empire frame, from the base at one side to the top on the opposite side.

The Process

1. Bind the frame and make a balloon lining (if required) – put it to one side.
2. Cut widths of fabric. In the example illustrated, the frame base has a circumference of 66cm and there are 6 struts. Therefore the strut gaps are 11cm.
3. Allow three times the fabric (66cm × 3 = 198cm) plus turns of 1cm, which gives 200cm. You can cut widths to add up to this amount, ensuring 1cm is left for each turning, but work them between struts. Also allow a 5cm contingency, so 205cm.
4. The height of the fabric will be more than usual because it will be positioned diagonally across the frame. The amount will be the measurement between one base ring strut and the point where the first pin will go at the top ring. Therefore decide how many struts you wish to move across – usually two or three – plus 6cm handling allowance.

This cotton fabric (by Molly Mahon) has been knife pleated at the base, and then swathed up and across two struts, matching the direction of the silk, positioned on the bias, in the sewn-on interlining.

The chiffon fabric here has been gathered between the two base struts and then swathed and pulled over halfway across the frame, that is, three of the six struts.

5. Mark the fabric with pencil/chalk along the top and base, showing the amount that needs to fit between each strut. Turn under 1cm at the end and pin it on the base ring, leaving a 3cm handling allowance.

6. If you decide to pleat the fabric, follow the instructions for making pleated lampshades earlier in this chapter; however, ensure these pleats are downwards facing (this stops dust getting in them), and this time pleat on the base ring first between two struts, before attaching them to the top ring individually. Pin in place. If gathering, use running stitch between two base struts, then pull and gather, and pin in place.

7. Now pull the first pleat or gather of the fabric gently and swathe it up and across to the chosen top ring strut. Pin in place. Pull up each pleat in turn to the top and make them smaller than the base pleats so that they fit in the space; pin in place.

8. If gathering the fabric, pull the fabric and pin at the end of each of the relevant two struts, gather by running stitch, and pin in place.

9. Now hand sew this first section of fabric at the base and then on the top ring, pulling up to ensure each pleat or gather tightly hugs the frame.

10. Repeat around the frame, pinning and sewing in place.

Note that if you are using chiffon or other very thin fabric, it is best to gather it on the frame using running stitch instead of using the sewing machine method, and use very small stitches when sewing.

Sunray Lampshades

Sunray lampshades have gathered fabric sewn around a section of or half of a frame. The fabric is ruched and drawn into a small circle, which is then positioned onto the centre of the frame (or elsewhere, you can decide if you have it at the base, for example, as an alternative). This central tightly gathered point will need covering, as the fabric will bunch up and have cut edges. It can be covered with a button or a handmade design, such as the rose trim (*see* Chapter 8). Very fine fabric, such as chiffon or other thin silks, is the best to use because of the tight gathering. As with gathered layered lampshades, these have an undercover that has been tailored to fit the frame. A balloon lining is then fitted to hide the metal of the frame, as well as the stitches made by attaching the centre of the outer fabric to the undercover.

This sunray pleated lampshade has been made by Elizabeth Pegg of Silkworm and Cottontails, bringing new life into a traditional style with modern fabrics.

The Process

For this example, the frame is a bowed empire with sunray pleating on each side.

1. First, bind the frame around the top and base rings and two opposite side struts (to be kept on permanently).
2. Make a balloon lining and put it to one side.
3. Place an undercover on the outside of the frame, either in two sections – sewn onto the side struts and around the rings – or as per the traditional tailored lampshades in Chapter 5.
4. Place a pencil mark in the centre of this cover. This will be the point where the central gather will be positioned, so measure from the sides, top, and base carefully for a true central position.
5. The height of the fabric required is calculated from the pencil-marked middle point to the base ring strut at the side of the frame – plus add on a working allowance of 5cm.
6. To obtain the width of fabric required and where it will be placed, measure around half of the frame – the example in the image has these combined half measurements:
   a. Top ring half = 15.7cm (half of the circumference).
   b. Base ring half = 31.4cm (half of the circumference).
   c. Side struts = 15cm each.
   d. Therefore the total is 77.1cm – round down to 77cm.
   e. Mark points around this half of the frame at four points – divide the 77cm by 4, which = 19.25cm.

7. Use the measurement of 77cm to work out how much fabric to use – three times will give 231cm. Divide this by 4, which = 57.75cm. This will be the amount to fit in between the four marks on the frame.
8. On a table, place the piece or pieces of fabric face up and mark or use tailor's tacks on it for the four sections of 57.75cm. Now sew small running stitches along one long edge just 5mm in. If you are joining widths of fabric, just use the needle to connect them as you sew the running stitches along, but ensure the cut edges are turned under slightly. Then pull the needle and thread so that the fabric gathers up and makes the tight knot/circle.
9. Attach this to the marked centre of the lampshade by hand stitching it onto the undercover as neatly as you can.
10. Then pull the cover fabric outwards and pin the edges of the four sections of fabric to the marks made on the frame.
11. Gather by eye the fabric between the four points and pin in place as you go. You can pleat as well, but this is dependent on the fabric used, as it may be bulky – try a sample to see how it lays.
12. Stitch the fabric in place (here, white thread is used for demonstration, but matching colour is best) and trim away the excess. The motif is then placed and sewn on to cover the central stitched circle. Repeat on the other side of the frame, and put in the balloon lining. Bias trim can be added to the side struts and then around the top and base rings.

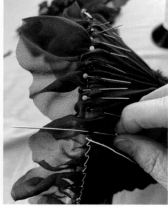

The key steps for making a sunray lampshade: sewing running stitches along the horizontal edges of the fabrics, joining widths; attaching the gathered central point to the centre of the lampshade's undercover; gathering or pleating the fabric on the frame and pinning it in place; hand stitching the fabric around the frame.

Choose a button or other covering to be placed over the central gathered fabric point, or hand make a motif.

Fan pleated lampshades have separate sections of fabric pulled tightly together at a top strut and then pleated to fit between a section of the base ring. This is then repeated the other way up and so forth around the frame.

Fan Pleated Lampshades

Straight sided frames are used to make fan pleated lamp-shades – wide oval frames or French drums are ideal, as there is less of a difference in size between the top and base rings (unlike an empire). Also, the strut positions at the top of the frame can be where the tightly gathered fabric points can be positioned.

The Process

1. Bind your top and base rings and two opposite side struts.
2. Make a balloon lining and either fit it in advance or put it to one side to fit later on.
3. Add an interlining if you are using a very thin or fine fabric such as chiffon (which suits this style best as the fabric has to be pulled closely together), or simply allow the pleated outer cover to hide the metal struts.
4. Measure the gap between two base struts. In the example in the images of the pink lampshade overleaf, the gap between the base struts is 16cm. Therefore the required amount of fabric is 3 × 16cm = 48cm, or 2.5 × 16cm = 40cm; make a sample to see which fits best. The height will be that of the frame plus a handling allowance.

After a section of fabric has been pinched together at a top strut, it is pleated at the base ring section.

The method is then repeated upside down around the frame, giving the name fan pleated lampshade.

5. In pencil, mark the midpoint between each base ring strut on the binding tape (so 8cm).

6. Pin the fabric on the top ring at a strut, each end of the width, and pinch it together into a really small bunch. Then stitch it close together and onto the bound ring.

7. Then pin the fabric onto the base ring, into the 16cm gap (8cm either side of the marked pencil point); pleat it by hand, and then pin each one in place, turning the ends under so as not to have a raw edge. Then hand sew it in place, but leave a small space at each end so that the next piece of fabric can be tucked just underneath it.

8. Now turn the frame and do the opposite, that is, pleated at the top ring between two struts and then taken to the base ring to a central marked point below. The pleats will be smaller here, as the top ring is less wide, so tuck the fabric neatly underneath.

9. Repeat all around, trim away the handling allowance, and add the balloon lining and trim to complete.

Always test samples of fabric to see if they will gather well to fit in place. Reduce the amount of fabric if needed to 2 or 2.5 × the base strut gap.

- If the gathers become loose after sewing on the cover, this can happen because the frame and therefore the cover are handled a lot. Before adding the trims, sew a few stitches between gathers at the base, pull down, and sew into the frame ring stitches – make sure it is within the 1cm to be hidden under the trim.
- If you have pinned the cover in place and leave it for a while (for example the next day) before sewing it, you may need to re-pin it to pull up the cover – it tends to relax if left.
- If the gathers or pleats appear to go 'off' to one side or the other, ensure you only sew the cover on after you have checked the vertical gathers or pleats are upright.
- If the thread keeps getting stuck around the pins and makes sewing difficult, either use short-length threads or pin and sew between one strut and the next instead of around the whole ring.
- Avoid snipping into the outer cover when trimming away the handling allowance of the lining after sewing it in place – lift the lining at a 90-degree angle to the frame. This will guide your scissors away from the outer fabric.
- If the bias binding is slipping up and showing the stitches, this is because there is a lot of fabric bunched together at the top, and sometimes this can push against the base of the bias trim after it has been sewn around the top. Either slip stitch around the base of the bias, catching in a couple of threads of the outer cover (under the bias) or run a smear of textile glue underneath to hold it in place.
- Always make small samples by working out the amount of fabric needed between two struts, cutting that amount, and then hand gathering it. Pin it onto the frame and see how it looks – it may look great around the base but barely fit between the top struts. This will help avoid expensive mistakes!

If the cover becomes loose or baggy after sewing, thread a needle and catch a thread of fabric, and connect some gathers around the base; pull down and sew into the base ring stitches.

CHAPTER 7

FURTHER IDEAS FOR SOFT LAMPSHADES

REMOVEABLE COVER LAMPSHADES

For these lampshades, covers are made and slipped over either a full frame or a pre-made hard lampshade, usually an empire or French drum in shape. They can be made using a variety of fabrics, can be lined or not, and you can add various trims, especially to the gathered slip covers. There are three main types included here: kitchen, gathered slipcover, and box pleated slipcover.

Kitchen Lampshades

These lampshades are so called as they were originally used to add more light while working in the kitchen, and were practical because the covers were removeable for hand-washing. These days, they are lovely decorative lampshades for anywhere in the home.

The Process

The slip cover has elasticated channels around the top and base edges. These are pulled tight to create small openings that are positioned on the top of and underneath a full frame. The cover is made by effectively creating a 'bag', and as they are shapeless, the fabric is clinched in with a decorative ribbon near the top of the frame, both giving form and creating the gathers. These are easy to make; they use little fabric and can be made in small sizes to really large for standard lamps. Simply enlarge the sizes given to suit your frame.

Note that these suit thinner fabrics such as lawns, cottons, or fine linens, which can be paired with a thin lining fabric. Thicker fabrics will struggle to gather around the drawn top casing, unless they are made unlined. For these lampshades, the fabric is not gathered too much as it can look bulky around the base ring, plus there is more to gather into the top smaller opening. The best frames to use are bowed empires, or even better, ones with a top collar fitting for the trim to be positioned around.

'Silver Grey Silk Kitchen Style Lampshade' beautifully made by Amanda Wheatland of Wyre & Gimble.

The completed kitchen lampshade, made with a Liberty Tana Lawn fabric, is fully lined and has the gathers held in with a velvet ribbon trim.

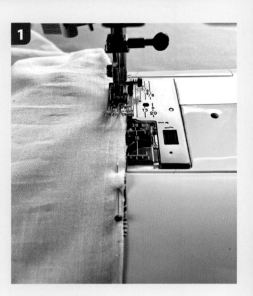

Pin the outer and lining fabrics face sides together, and machine very small 5mm seams along the horizontal top and base lengths, leaving a 1cm gap or space at each end. Then machine down one vertical side, starting 1cm down and ending 1cm before the end. These gaps are open so the elastic can be fitted inside later.

Lined Kitchen Lampshade

First work out the amount of fabric needed:

- The cover needs to be large enough height-wise to go over the frame and then extend towards the middle of the top and base of it.
- The measurements need to be planned in relation to the size of the frame being used: for smaller frames, allow around 3–5cm to go over the rings; allow more for larger frames.
- Note that you will not end up with that exact amount, as the fabric is pinched into the gathers, plus they will be pulled a little when the trim is added. Note also that the smaller the hole you opt for, the tighter the gathers will be.

First Steps

For this tutorial, a lined cover is made using cotton lawn fabric, and the frame is a bespoke bowed empire scallop frame with the following dimensions:

- top diameter = 10cm

- base diameter = 20cm; circumference = 62.8cm, rounded up to 63cm
- frame height = 18.5cm.

Fabric Amount

Work out the fabric requirement in relation to the base ring:

- The circumference is 63cm, plus add on 1cm each end for seams, plus more for the gather.
- The fabric width is therefore base circumference (63cm) + seams (1cm each end = 2cm) + gather (7cm) = 72cm.
- The fabric height will be the frame (18.5cm) + top turning (3.5cm) + base turning (4.5cm) + 1.5cm each for top and base channels = 30cm (rounded up; this extra will be lost in height when the fabric is gathered up).

First cut the fabric 72cm × 30cm and then cut a piece of lining fabric the same size. Here, curtain lining is used, but you can use any thin fabric to line your lampshade. Iron the fabrics smooth, then lay them on the table face/right sides together. Follow the tutorial to make a lined kitchen lampshade:

Machine down the other short side but this time leave open a central gap of around 10cm. Then turn the 'bag' inside out through this 10cm gap – you will see that the top and base seams stitches are hidden within. Then hand sew, with small slip stitches, the 10cm (4in) opening you made.

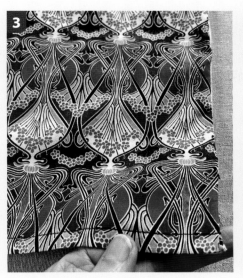

Now make the casings along the top and base horizontals – this is the long channel where the elastic will be threaded through and positioned. Machine along the lengths (using matching colour threads) 1cm down from the top and base edges, ensuring you leave the 1cm spaces at each end still open. Press the fabric and lay it flat on the table.

First put the elastic through the base channel of the fabric – take a length of elastic (anything 3–7mm wide) and place a safety pin in one end of it; pin that to the fabric (this stops it being pulled down into the channel). Attach the other end of the elastic to a bodkin, or another closed long safety pin, and push this inside and along the channel.

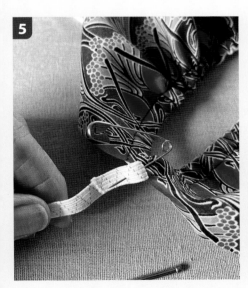

The fabric will gather as you progress. When you reach the end, holding both ends of the elastic firmly, take the elastic off the bodkin and the other end off the safety pin. Now pin both these ends together with the safety pin, being careful not to let go of the ends! Then do the same along the top edge channel.

Next, place the cover onto the frame and manoeuvre it into the right position. When central, free one end of the elastic around the top, and pull it until the cover has a small hole – it will probably be around 4cm in diameter. Then re-attach the safety pin to the elastic, keeping the ends tightly together. Repeat with the base ring. Take the cover off and hand sew the pieces of elastic tape together where pinned, using small stitches. Trim off the ends, and tuck tape into the channel; now sew the ends together, folding under any raw edges.

Place the cover on the frame and position it so it sits centrally over. You can slip stitch the vertical open seam, but it should get lost in the gathers in the fabric. Now add a length of ribbon or other trim – place it around near the top of the frame, pull to clinch the gathers, and pin. Then remove the ribbon and make small stitches, adding a button if you wish. Then place it back over the outer cover. Your lampshade is complete.

Slipcover Lampshades

Slipcovers for lampshades can also be made. A circle of fabric is created, either lined or unlined, by machine joining two short sides of a rectangle; this can then either be gathered or box pleated to fit on top of a full frame or onto a pre-made hard lampshade.

Linings

If the cover is being placed onto a pre-made or bought hard lampshade, this will act as the lining. However, if you are using a frame, the slipcovers can be made either unlined or lined:

- The lining and main fabric can be paired together to make the cover as one – this is a good idea if the fabric being used is thin, such as cotton lawn, or if you need more structure as in the box pleated style.
- You can add a balloon lining in advance; however, the cut edges and stitches would be seen when looking into the lampshade. It is therefore preferable to cover the rings with a matching or contrasting bias binding, either after adding a fixed balloon lining or simply to hide the metalware rings. You could also spray paint the frame to match the fabric colour if preferred.

The tutorials here outline how to make both unlined and lined versions of the covers, but you can make your own versions and styles including adding trims, adding more height to have more channels or pleats, or using different frames.

Gathered Slipcover

These lampshades have fabric covers using three times the circumference measurement of the top ring. A circle of fabric is created by seaming the short edges of the rectangle of fabric. Channels are then created in the top section, and lengths of elastic or ribbon pulled through to be gathered – this allows a snug fit. For the tutorial, the cover is the unlined version; *see* detail on making one with a lining in the 'Box Pleated Slipcover' section.

The gathered slipcover lampshade, made using cotton fabric that has been gathered around the top. It can then sit either onto a full frame or a pre-made hard lampshade.

The frame used in the tutorial is a French drum with the following dimensions:

- top ring = 6in/15.5cm diameter; circumference rounded down to 48cm
- base ring = 8in/20.5cm diameter
- height = 6in/15.5cm.

The quantity of fabric (three times) to be used is worked out in relation to the top ring:

- Top ring circumference = 48cm.
- × 3 = 144cm, plus 1cm each end for the seam = 146cm (or join two pieces, each 72cm, add 1cm onto each end for the seams; machine this and match pattern if relevant).
- Height of fabric = frame (15.5cm) + 10cm for top turnings and 7cm for base plus extra to hide frame (5cm) = 37.5cm.

To make the slipcover, a circle of fabric is made – cut the fabric the correct size and press it, and then lay it onto the table, pattern side or face side down. Now follow the tutorial.

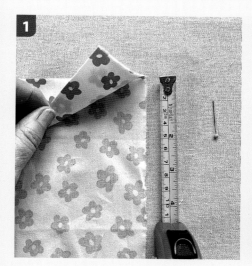

Fold towards you 5cm along the top width of the fabric, and then fold it over another 5cm again, giving you a 5cm top hem. Pin and press in place. Having this doubled hem gives structure, as the slipcover is not going to be lined. Then fold up the base seam, again doubled, but this time 3.5cm all along.

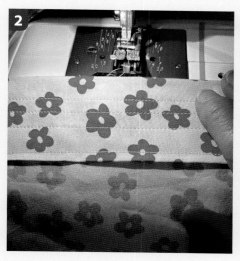

Machine along the top horizontal length of the fabric – the measurements you want for your channels. Here we have 1.5cm down from the edge, then 1cm, another 1cm and then 1.5cm, ensuring the lines are parallel. If you wish to have more of a header, or add more channels, increase the size of cut fabric for the top.

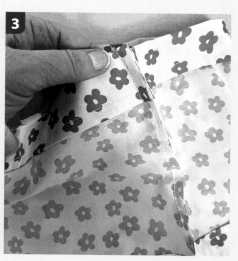

Pin and then machine along the base hem, or slip stitch if preferred – you can check the length at this stage to your liking. Then machine the short sides of the rectangle together, 1cm in from the cut edges. You now have the circle of fabric machined to the correct size (Note: you can also box pleat this circle, with 4cm pleats, as an unlined cover, which will fit the same frame.)

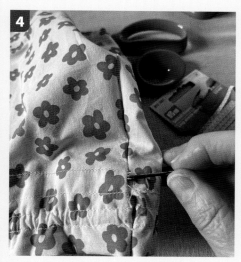

When machining down the side seam, you can allow openings for the channels, but it is easier to simply unpick the relevant threads where you wish the elastic or ribbon to enter the channels, and then re-stitch after making the slipcover. Use a stitch ripper/unpicker for this.

Take a length of elastic or ribbon and attach one end of it to the fabric with a safety pin. Attach the other end to a bodkin or safety pin, thread it through the channel, and push it all along. At the end, tie the ends but do not pull at this stage. Repeat for other channels if you wish. When completed, place the cover on the frame and pull to fit tightly. Sew the ends of elastic or ribbon together as well as the ends of the channels.

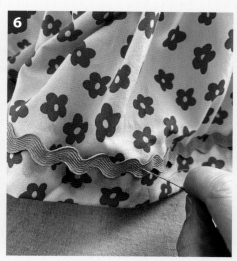

You can decorate your loose gathered slipcover with different kinds of trims, from ribbon to a frill trim (see Chapter 8), but here a length of ricrac in a different colour is attached. Hand sew using small stitches in matching thread. Turn under the ends; this will hide the machine stitching used to sew the base hem. The lampshade is now complete – simply pop the cover onto the frame.

Box Pleated Slipcover

The box pleated slipcover can be positioned over either a pre-made hard lampshade or a lampshade frame. As per the gathered slipcover above, this box pleated cover is also made by creating a circle of fabric, and then box pleating it to size. However, because each pleat needs to be uniform in size, there are calculations to be worked out in advance, and therefore the fabric circle dimension is made to accommodate them.

If you wish to have an unlined cover, after working out the maths, cut the fabric as per the tuition for the gathered slipcover, making the circle of fabric, and then join this tuition here at step 3. The tutorial here shows you the method for making the box pleated slipcover with a lining.

Choose the size of frame you wish to have. In the tutorial, the frame is a French drum with the same dimensions as the gathered lampshade above, and therefore the width of fabric will be the same requirement as we work to three times the fullness. Consider the pattern should you wish to factor it into the pleat itself (for example stripes or check sizes can be calculated) or if you have more than one width of fabric.

Careful consideration needs to be given to the amount of fabric needed, as box pleats are precise:

- The pleats will be 4cm wide and we will use 3 × the amount of fabric, so 12cm for each pleat.
- There are 6 struts, each having 2 pleats, which gives 12 pleats in total × 12cm fabric = 144cm, plus 1cm seams.
- If the fabric width is narrower than this, either railroad it or cut two pieces of 72cm, plus 1cm seams for each piece, which means each piece of fabric = 74cm (width); you can then join them to be one length.
- The height required = frame (15.5cm) + top header (5cm × 2 = 10cm) + 1cm folded under, plus base fold (3.5cm × 2 = 7cm) + 1cm folded under, plus extra to hide frame (5cm) = 39.5cm minimum cut height.
- The lining amount needed is width as above, and height as above less 5cm from the top and 3.5cm from the base.

The completed box pleated slipcover lampshade, which is lined, and fits neatly onto a lampshade frame or a pre-made hard lampshade.

The fabric quantities are exact above, but of course fabric can be stretched a little when being handled. Before you machine the box pleats (*see* step 4 of tutorial), lay the cover onto the lampshade frame you will be using and check it will sit firmly. If not, tweak the pleats (but all the same size) to accommodate, or sew small stitches from the cover into a bound frame.

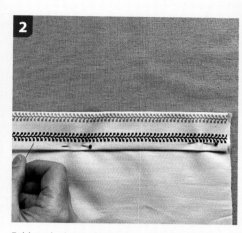

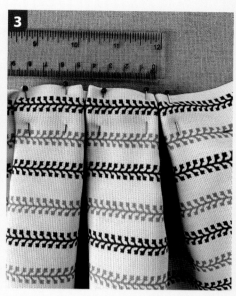

Lay the pressed fabric face down and turn over 5cm towards you from the top horizontal length; then tuck and press 1cm of it underneath to hide the raw edge. Then put the lining under this fold, the top of which will be in the crease of the outer fabric. Place pins all along the edge of the fabric and then slip stitch along the length of folded fabric, just picking up the lining.

Fold up the base of the fabric – 3.5cm and then again for a double seam, which gives form to the pleats. Tuck the lining under, to the edge of the fabric, and then turn 1cm of the main fabric under for a neat edge. Either machine along the base edge 1cm up from the edge or use slip stitch if preferred – this will give a clean look with no stitches visible.

Face sides together, machine the short vertical edges of the fabric 1cm in from the cut edges – this will make the circle. Start at the seam and hide the stitches behind the first pleat; using a ruler to ensure accuracy, make the box pleats – the first underneath part will be 2cm folded under, then under the front 4cm box pleat will be the next 2cm. Continue around the circle you have made.

Pin all the pleats in place, and then put it on the sewing machine and carefully machine 3cm down from the top of the cover along the pleats, ensuring they are all captured in and meet each other. Then machine another line of stitches 1cm below, ensuring the lines are parallel, and again that the pleats are touching. You may find they can slip away from each other while machining, you can add small hand stitches afterwards if helpful.

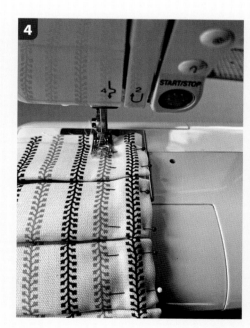

Take the cover off the machine and place on an ironing board. Now press the pleats carefully all the way around the top. You can either have formal pleats, where they are pressed into firm pleats all the way down (as here), or you can have a relaxed look, only pressing the top and leaving the base edges loose and more gathered. Place the finished cover onto the frame or hard lampshade.

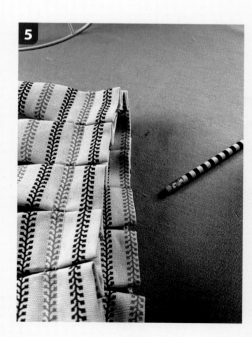

REMAKING TRADITIONAL LAMPSHADES

There are so many different styles, shapes, and sizes of lampshade frame, many of which came along with the lamp base they were partnered with. A well-made hand sewn lampshade should last a good ten years at least; unfortunately, however, there were times when high-wattage bulbs were used, resulting in the scorching of the lining, and even the outer cover. That said, it is absolutely worth remaking these lampshades. As mentioned in the 'Remaking Hard Lampshades' section in Chapter 3:

- Recycling and repurposing is always good – throwing metal away is not kind to the environment.
- The newly covered lampshade will wish to be with its original base for a perfect pairing, size-wise and decoratively.
- It is cost effective with the small amount of fabric used.

The Process

You can either make the lampshades like for like, or source another fabric in a different colourway or pattern. Vintage frames can be sourced from charity shops, vintage markets, online auctions, or auction houses, and sometimes a wonderful lampshade will be passed over because of the tired cover – it is worth breathing new life into it by giving it a remake. Note that:

- It is always good to remake the whole lampshade; trying simply to replace a lining does not really work, as the outer cover can become overhandled and damaged.
- It may be the binding tape that has relaxed, or become rusty, and has resulted in the cover and lining becoming baggy – therefore it needs a complete remake.

Made by Helen Kenning at Glow Lampshades, this lampshade has been expertly restored in the traditional way; the frame was stripped down and treated for rust, new silk and lining was sourced, and the original lace reused, all hand sewn into place.

First Steps

1. Strip down the outer cover and any linings. Carefully take off any trims – you may wish to reuse these.
2. Check the frame for any changes in its shape – it needs to be robust, so no cracks where the struts meet the rings, and symmetrical, not bent.
3. Check also for rust and chips off the original paint. If there are issues, use a large file to rub it down, or even completely strip it of paint, and then place in a box outside and re-spray using PlastiKote paint in a colour of your choice (white for lined and any colour you wish for unlined).
4. Then make the lampshade using the techniques outlined in this book – whether traditional stretched, gathered, or pleated, you will be able to remake the lampshade using the methods shown.

Note that you may find that the original cover was glued or that the binding is still there; however, it is always best to re-bind and not use glue on frames – it is one of the reasons they need remaking!

Collect vintage lampshades and give them a new lease of life. 'Lily' the car kindly lent by Frank Warren. (PHOTO: CAITLIN WARREN)

HELPFUL HINTS FOR SOFT TAILORED LAMPSHADE MAKING SUCCESS

- Make absolutely sure that your binding on the frame is completely unyielding – any movement will mean your cover may start becoming baggy too.
- For traditional tailored lampshades, make sure the two halves of the fabric you use follow exactly the same grain lines – if the angles are different, they will fight against each other and your cover will not be a good fit.
- Check there are no loose threads between the lining and the cover; you will see them when the lampshade is lit.
- Ensure all your stitches for both the cover and the lining are on the front of the rings of the frame, not the top; otherwise they will not be hidden by your trim, and will show under the lining too.
- If your cover will not fit exactly flat regardless of how many times you stretch it, follow the grain of fabric direction, then take out pins on the side struts, re-pull, and re-pin.
- If the silk on your lampshade becomes baggy as you stretch it,

place it under the steam of a kettle so it pings back in place.
- Pinholes in the fabric can also be eradicated with kettle steam.
- If you prick yourself and your blood goes on the fabric, use your own saliva (on a piece of fabric) to rub it away – it works!
- Try samples of your fabrics and linings together in front of a light bulb to check the appearance before you start making it – they can look very different lit up.
- Always use LED bulbs; they are cool to the touch to prevent scorching.
- Spray the inside of your lampshade with a fire-proofing spray just to be on the safe side.
- Take your time to make your lampshades – they are a slow interiors, soft furnishings item, and need precision and care.
- Place your lampshades out of direct sunshine; it fades the fabric and can rot silk.
- Finally, experiment with fabrics, trims, and linings – the options are endless!

CHAPTER 8

TRIMS FOR LAMPSHADES

TRIM THE LIGHT FANTASTIC!

There are so many beautiful trims available, ranging from simple braids and cords to diamante, feathers, and glass bead ornate trims – the choice seems endless. Narrow down the options by deciding if the job of the trim is simply to hide the stitching (on hand sewn lampshades) or if you want the trim to be the star of the show. For example, a simple plain grey stretched fabric on a lovely shaped frame can take on a new life with a complex and brightly coloured trim, whereas a lampshade made using a highly patterned fabric may simply need a modest braid to cover the stitches. Because some of the bought trims have an unfinished edging to which the main trim is attached – such as beads on ribbon – you can place a strip of bias binding on top of the ribbon to hide its pulled edges.

As well as buying ready-made trims, it is possible to commission bespoke, complex, handmade items from specialist passementerie workshops – including dyeing, cord-spinning, weaving, and tassel-making to your specification. There are also companies who will create a range of trims to your own designs, or using their designs but in your choice of colourways.

You can also make your own trims, using and manipulating ribbon or fabric fashioned into something sensational. By following the tutorials in this chapter, you will learn how to pleat, make ruffles and double ruffles, and more, using either lengths of fabric or ribbon.

Dip-dye bespoke fringes by Jessica Light. All Jessica's trims are hand woven and hand made to order in her East London workshop.

A plain grey lampshade has added opulence with this colourful trim from V V Rouleaux.

Handmade trims can add a truly bespoke design to a lampshade by using the outer fabric and shaping it into something special. Lampshade and trim made by Elizabeth Pegg of Silkworm and Cottontails, showcasing her wonderful ruched and box pleated trim.

TRIMS FOR HARD LAMPSHADES

Because fabric and paper have been adhered onto laminate material to make hard lampshades, it is difficult to hand sew trims onto them. However, by using textile glue, a glue gun, or double-sided tape, you can add a lovely choice of trims onto hard lampshades. They particularly look good with a long silky fringe, some velvet edging, or simply a plain Petersham ribbon, which can be ironed or smoothed over the rings.

Bias binding is used extensively with hard lampshades made using paper that need to have their cut edges hidden. *See* later in this chapter for how to make this, and Chapter 2 for attaching it to hard lampshades.

It is possible to add a trim to the inside of the lampshade. However, if the light fitting is positioned on the base ring, and is to be placed on a lamp base, then the gimbals will be in the way. In this case, it is preferable to make your lampshade using a duplex fitting (*see* 'Ring Sets and Fittings' in Chapter 1) so that the ring is uncluttered and able to have the trim attached inside it.

To add trims to hard lampshades, simply add a strip of double-sided tape around the base ring (starting at the seam), take off the cover, and add the trim to it, slowly pressing down as you go. Alternatively use textile glue to attach the trim. Turn under the cut edges at the start and end at the seam so there are no raw edges/fraying.

TRIMS FOR SOFT HAND SEWN LAMPSHADES

Because traditional soft lampshades are hand sewn, the stitches created are visible on the front of the top and base rings. Therefore trims have a practical role to hide them, as well as being decorative. It is advantageous to use a material that has some stretch – it has to be worked around the curves of the ring, and even rectangular and square lampshades have rounded-edged frames, so it needs to be flexible enough to hug the curves. However, you can use one trim, such as bias binding, to hide the stitches and then another more decorative one on top of it to add character.

There are lots of trims available either online or in shops, including a huge variety from V V Rouleaux, perfect for lampshades.

Petersham ribbon adds a lovely finish to hard lampshades. It can be shaped by ironing and easily smoothed over and adhered to the rings.

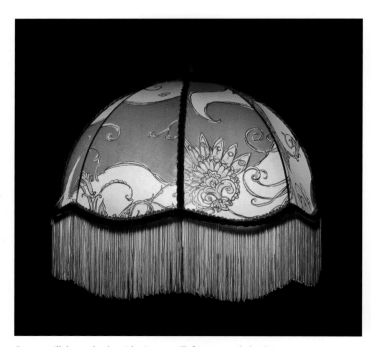

Orange silk lampshade with vintage silk fringe, made by Fringe Handcrafted Lampshades.

This vintage original lampshade from the 1950s has an extravagant silk bobble trim around the base and simple gimp braid around the top.

As well as finding wonderful trims online or in specialist shops, you can also look out for classic hand sewn lampshade trims by sourcing genuine vintage examples from the 1920s–50s. They are often very luxurious and complex although they maybe limited in colours.

HAND MAKING LAMPSHADE TRIMS

There are advantages to hand making trims:

- You can incorporate the outer fabric or match the lining colour to the design of the lampshade.
- Although it is more time consuming, it is more cost effective.
- You are creating something truly bespoke, giving a made-to-measure finish to the lampshade.

Bias Binding

Bias binding is used extensively in lampshade making for both soft and hard lampshades. It is possible to join lengths to save on fabric quantities, but it can look better with only one vertical seam. Advantages of making and using your own bias binding include:

- It is neat and has stretch, so can be positioned easily around the curves of the rings.

Making bias binding in a complementary colour to that of the outer cover brings the design together, and hand making it ensures correct widths, texture, and colour choice.

- It hides all the stitching on hand sewn lampshades.
- It is straightforward to make, and although you can buy it online and from shops in all widths and colours, generally speaking it is better if you can make your own, as you will be using better base cloth, matching colours, and texture. If you have used a rich linen for the outer cover, why use thin cotton bias to complete it?
- Shop-bought bias binding also tends to be less stretchy, which can cause issues with application.
- It neatly brings order to gathered and pleated lampshades, which invariably look messy with their cut edges.
- Making your own ensures you can choose the width of binding you wish to have – the larger the frame, the wider the bias used.

For attaching bias binding to hard lampshades, please *see* Chapter 2 for instruction. For attaching bias binding to soft lampshades – both lined and unlined – please *see* both methods in Chapter 5.

Making Bias Binding

The following tutorial shows two methods to make bias binding: first by using a bias maker and second by hand. Bias makers only come in certain width sizes, and you may wish to have a different size and will therefore make it differently. In both cases, first measure the base and top circumferences of the lampshade, and add 2cm allowance for the length needed.

Suggested width sizes of bias bindings for lampshades are:

- hard lampshades – 15mm
- hand sewn lampshades – 12mm for lined small/medium lampshades; 15mm for medium/larger lampshades; 18mm for unlined lampshades.

However, you can choose the width you prefer, and make it using the methods described here.

First Steps

First learn how to find the bias on your fabric – please refer to Chapter 4 for detail and the images showing you how to find the bias on fabric.

The following tutorials demonstrate how to make 12mm bias binding using a bias binding maker, and 15mm bias binding by hand.

To make bias binding, you will need:

- self-healing cutting mat or a table with protective cover
- rotary cutter or sharp fabric scissors
- grid rule or tape measure
- pencil or tailor's chalk
- bias binding maker
- fabric of your choice.

Place the mat and materials on a large table for cutting and have an iron and ironing board to hand, as this will be used to make the bias binding. There are small portable irons available, which work well for making trims; however, ensure you have a protective cover on top of the cutting mat to avoid warping.

Collect together the tools and materials needed to make bias binding.

TUTORIAL: USING A BIAS BINDING MAKER

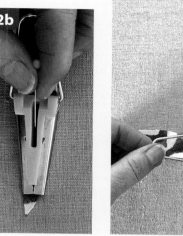

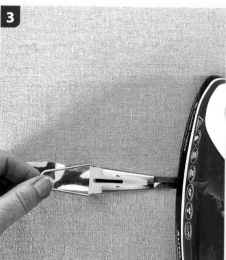

Cut the fabric on the bias, the cut width being twice the size of the finished binding width; therefore to make this 12mm bias, 24mm (or rounded up to 25mm if easier) is required and the length you wish to have (plus 2cm seam allowance). Do this on a self-healing mat if using a rotary cutter. Keep an angled end to the strip.

On an ironing board or mat protector, feed one angled end of the cut strip, face/pattern side down, into the maker. Use a pin to help draw the fabric through if needed. Make sure the fabric is sitting exactly around the maker so there is the same amount either side coming out.

Use the handle on the maker to pull the fabric slowly as it comes through it, and use the iron to press the folded-in edges – these should meet exactly in the middle. Keep the iron at right angles to the maker, otherwise it will go into the strip and reopen it. When completed, snip away the angled ends.

TUTORIAL: MAKING BIAS BINDING BY HAND

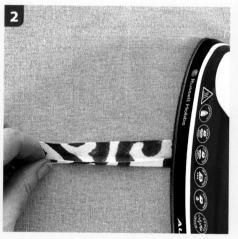

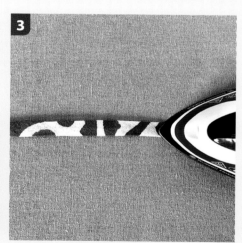

Cut out the amount of fabric needed. Here, the finished bias width will be 15mm, therefore 30mm width × the length you wish (plus 2cm seam allowance). You will not need an angled end. Place the fabric face/pattern side down and fold it in half so that the horizontal edges meet; iron together.

This will create a pressed line exactly down the middle of the strip. Now open the fabric up (still face/pattern side down) and turn up one cut edge to the middle, meeting the ironed line. Then press it all along the horizontal.

Repeat on the other side, ensuring the two cut edges meet exactly in the middle. Turn the strip over and iron out the middle pressed line. Using a steam iron helps with this. The bias is now ready to attach around the lampshade.

Handmade Decorative Trims

If a complex pleated lampshade has been made, a simple finish such as bias binding is often chosen so as not to detract from the main design. For some lampshades, however, it is the trim that is the key decorative feature.

Trims can be made using either:

- Ribbon – this is easier to work with as it does not have raw edges and can be of high quality, although it does not have any stretch.
- The outer fabric, or any cut fabric – the trims are fashioned from being made into a 'tube' – this avoids fraying, although you can use the raw cut edges to good decorative effect too (*see* tutorial).

The fabric tube or ribbon can then be manipulated into lots of different styles of trims – pleated, box pleated, ruched, and so on. As a rule, use three times the circumference of the base ring, with a 'square' height. For example, each box pleat could be 2.5cm wide using a 2.5cm high ribbon or tube. However this is personal choice, so make small samples in advance to achieve the best proportions for your frame and achieve the look you want. Note that it is best to avoid bias binding if making a trim such as box pleated, as the cut back edges will open up.

Follow these step-by-step instructions to hand make trims for using either fabric tubes or ribbon.

Box Pleated Trims

Getting Started

Work out how many pleats will fit evenly around the base ring and what size you want them to be in proportion to the frame:

- The bespoke 20cm frame used here has a circumference of 62.8cm, rounded to 63cm.

TUTORIAL: MAKING A FABRIC 'TUBE'

The tube is made by cutting the height of fabric twice the size of the required finished trim, plus 1cm for the seam. For example for a finished trim 2.5cm high:

1. Cut the fabric on the straight of grain, 6cm high for this example. The width will be three times the circumference of the base ring, plus 2cm seam allowance.
2. Place right/patterned long sides together, and machine sew 5mm in from the edge all along the horizontal edges. If you need a lot of fabric as a length, join lengths together first.

3. Turn the tube inside out: use a short length of cord, ribbon, or elastic and place one end in a bodkin or attach to a safety pin, and attach the other end to a safety pin, pinned to the fabric; then push the bodkin/safety pin inside through the sewn channel to the other end. By being attached it will turn the tube inside out.
4. You can also place a length of cord or ribbon in the inside of the channel, pinning it at one end of the opening, before machine sewing the seam, and then pulling it at the other end; this will turn the tube the right side out.
5. Place the machined seam at the back, in the middle of the tube, so it will not be seen on the lampshade. Iron it smooth and flat.

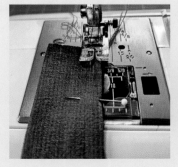   

Making a fabric tube allows neat edges, and it can then be formed into all kinds of handmade trims.

- It has 6 × strut gaps of 10.5cm.
- The pleats could be 3 of 3.5cm wide between each strut gap, or 4 of 2.62cm (rounded to 2.5cm). As the height of the trim being used is also 2.5cm, it makes sense for them to be 'square' in shape, and therefore the smaller size has been selected.

Follow the tutorial to make either straightforward box pleats, or to add to them with beads as 'butterfly' box trims. Ribbon has been used for clarity, but any patterned fabric tube or ribbon can be used for this trim.

The completed box pleated trim – it can be left as simple pleats or added to by creating butterfly pleats with added beads, as shown here.

TUTORIAL: MAKING BOX PLEATED TRIMS

Lay the ribbon or pressed fabric tube length on the table, and ensure the seam is positioned at the back in the middle if using a tube. Then leave 1cm at one end, and box pleat the fabric ensuring half pleats (1.25 cm) meet in the middle of the 2.5cm pleats at the front. You can make them by measuring using a ruler as you go, as opposed to making marks. Pin both sides of the pleat.

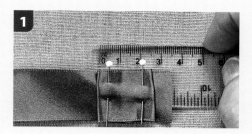

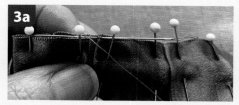

After making the first set of pleats (× 4 to fit between two struts), pin them to the lampshade to check for the size; tweak if necessary. Then take off again, lay the rest of the ribbon or tube on the table, and make the remainder of the box pleats. You can now either machine along the middle of the pleats – the stitching will show, but this will be hidden if having butterfly pleats – or you can hand sew, as shown in the next step.

To hand sew small stitches at the back and at the front of each pleat, connect each of them in turn, using matching colour thread and ensuring the thread knots are hidden behind or under the pleats; the stitches connect the pleats to each other. The trim is now ready to be stitched to the lampshade frame: use small stitches at the back to attach it, where the cover or lining stitches are on the frame, tucking under the ends for neatness.

Alternatively, you can make butterfly pleats – pinch together the middle of the top and base of the pleats and make a small stitch, using matching colour thread. You can add beads too, either all the same colour or a mix to add more interest. Then make small stitches (or use textile glue) to add the trim to the lampshade, sewing it on top of the main stitches underneath. Tuck the ends under for neatness.

Knife Pleated Trim

As with box pleats, the size of knife pleats needs to be planned before you start making the trim so they are the same size, neatly fitting around the base ring. You can use a fabric tube or a length of ribbon – three times the circumference of the base ring.

As for the frame size used for the box pleating tutorial, the circumference is 63cm; the ribbon used is 2.5cm, so there will be 4 × 2.5cm pleats between each strut. Again, ribbon has been used for clarity.

The completed knife pleated trim: these can be made using ribbon or a fabric tube, and can be touching or gap pleats (*see* Chapter 6 for detail).

TUTORIAL: MAKING KNIFE PLEATED TRIMS

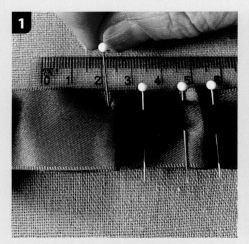

1

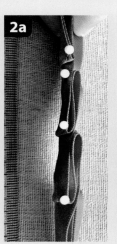

2a

2b

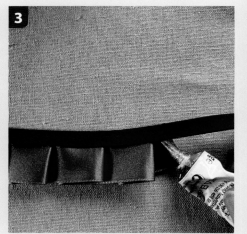

3

Lay the ribbon or fabric onto the table and leave 1cm at one end. Then using a ruler, pleat by hand the exact knife pleat sizes. These are 2.5cm wide, therefore fold the material under to the left, measuring as you go, ensuring the fabric touches at the back. Place pins in each side of the fold. Work along the length.

Check the pleats are touching at the back and are placed squarely; add more pins to keep them firmly in place. Then, using matching thread, machine along the top of the pleats 3mm in from the top edge, slowly and carefully, so as not to splay them open, and removing the pins as you go along.

Because the machine stitches will be on show, add a narrow band of bias binding to hide them; use textile glue to attach it. Now add the trim to the lampshade – either using small stitches at the back or textile glue – ensuring the trim is placed over the top of the main stitches underneath. Tuck the 1cm ends underneath for a neat finish.

Ruched Trim

Ruched ribbon or fabric trims have small running stitches placed along the long horizontal edges, either on the sewing machine or by hand, which are then pulled and gathered. Use three times the circumference of the base ring for a full ruche effect. Once made, turn under the first and last 1cm for neatness. Pin and either sew or glue onto the main stitches on the lampshade (revisit Chapter 6 to see this trim on a ruched lampshade). Note that you will lose a lot of height of the ribbon once it has been pulled, so be generous with the height choice.

Shell or Petal Edged Trim

The shell edged trim is made using running stitch on either ribbon or fabric – the stitches of which are placed in a 'v' shape along the length. When the thread is pulled, the edges of the material curl inwards and outwards. In the images shown here, contrasting thread has been used to show the direction of stitches; use matching thread when you make your own, and allow three times the circumference of the base ring. Note the ribbon width will either stay the same as it is pulled or even increase in size a little. Try out the size widths of the 'v' being used – there is no hard and fast rule – to see which effect you like the best, but do ensure you sew them all the same size. Here there are 5cm gaps at the end of the 'v's. It is helpful to pull the thread to gather as you go along. You can also layer different colours of shell edged trim on top to have a fuller effect.

Shell edged trims look sumptuous using shiny ribbon, but can also be made using fabric tube for a more three-dimensional, plumper effect.

Ribbon has been ruched along the horizontal edges of the ribbon, by hand stitching along the edges, the threads being pulled for a lovely gathered trim.

To make the shell edged trim, first make a 'v' shape using running stitch along the length of the fabric or ribbon.

Pull the threads along as you go to ruffle up the trim. A shell edged pattern will appear.

Ruffle Trims

Ruffle trims can be made using:

- a fabric tube or lengths of ribbon, both of which have neat edges
- strips of fabric or ribbon with raw edges to add to a decorative effect.

For a single ruffle, a line of machine stitches or hand sewn running stitches are sewn down the middle of the fabric or ribbon strips, and then pulled up to gather the material into a ruffle (this hides the middle stitches). However, for a fuller ruffle, try the 'double ruffle', a really lovely trim that suits both handmade gathered as well as stretched hand sewn lampshades.

There are a few tips to keep in mind:

- Cut the fabric using pinking shears/zigzag scissors, as this adds to the effect.
- Use three times the circumference of the lampshade base ring.
- Mark the strips of fabric in advance by dividing it equally by the number of struts you have. Alternatively, because it has such a relaxed look, you can do this by eye once ready to place onto the frame.
- Note that if you use a printed fabric with pattern only on the front, you will see the plain underside of it when it is ruffled. It therefore works best with a woven fabric.
- It also works well with silks, as the edges fray a little, adding to the ruffled look.

Follow the tutorial to make the double ruffle trim.

The completed double ruffle trim adds to the cottagecore-style look of this gingham gathered lampshade.

On a self-healing board, cut two strips of fabric three times the circumference of the base ring, joining lengths, and allow 1cm turnings for each end. Choose a height in proportion to the frame. Use pinking shears/zigzag scissors to get angled edges. Now lay one strip on top of the other and, using matching thread, sew running stitches down the middle of both pieces of fabric. Start 1cm in.

Gather and make the ruffles as you sew, and when completed, tweak the length so that it will fit snugly around the base ring, turning under the 1cm ends. Pin it in place, apportioning the ruffles so they are fairly distributed around, or matching your points with the struts. Using small stitches, sew the trim (in the middle of it) onto the base ring, on top of and hiding the stitches already there from making the lampshade.

Thread a fine needle with matching colour thread. Pinch together two pieces of the top layer of ruffled fabric – above and below the middle stitch line – and sew them together with a small stitch, hiding the knotted end underneath (or use textile glue if preferred). Move down another 1.5cm or as close as you wish, and repeat. Work your way all around until you have reached the end. Fold under the last 1cm for a neat edge.

Frilled Trims

These trims can be made either with rough cut edges, which gives an unstructured look that can really work with some lampshades, or with smooth edges for a neater look. For a smooth-edged trim, simply make a fabric tube, sew small stitches down one horizontal edge, and pull the thread to make it frill. They are best made using joined fabric rather than ribbon, simply because the thickness gives more structure. However, make samples in advance so that you achieve the look you want. Rough-edged frills can be left with their frayed edges (as per the tartan lampshade in the image), or you can cover the cut edge with bias binding as per the 'Rough-Edged Frilled Trim' tutorial. They can be made using two different fabrics, which adds interest, as the underside will curl upwards. You can then sew the frill onto the lampshade, covering the stitches made when sewing the cover and lining in place.

This lampshade has a rough-edged frilled trim. The cut edges add to the look achieved. It has the main fabric on the top and a grey silk underneath to add interest.

Rough-Edged Frilled Trim

The gathered lampshade made in Chapter 6 has a rough-edged frilled trim added around the base edge. This has then been neatened with bias binding around its top edge. For the tutorial, one piece of fabric is used, which will be folded in half. First, measure and cut the amount of fabric needed:

- 3 × the circumference of the base ring; for this 10in/25.5cm frame, circumference (80cm) × 3 = 240cm, plus 1cm each end side seam, so cut length is 242cm. Join lengths if needed.
- The height of the finished trim is 4cm high, therefore the cut strips are 8.5cm high (2.5mm allowance for each sewn edge).

Rough-Edged Frill: Two Fabrics

You can also make this trim using two different fabrics joined together. The advantage is that when it is pulled, and the frills curl, the under-fabric will be on show, and therefore it can be an eye-catching detail. The method is described in steps 1–3 in the 'Rose Trim' instructions opposite.

TUTORIAL: MAKING A ROUGH-EDGED FRILLED TRIM

Cut lengths of the trim needed and fold up the strip in half so you have just over 4cm. Press in along the length so it is closed. Lay the cut length on the table and place small marks at equal distances on the underside of the trim, so that it will get shared out equally around the frame: this has six struts and so there will be a mark every 40cm (240cm divided by 6), or you can do by eye if preferred.

Turn under the cut end edges inside the trim and, using single thread, make running stitch along the top cut edges of the strip of fabric. Pull the threads as you sew along – it is easier than leaving it until the end with long lengths. You can machine it if you prefer. Place the frame base up on the table and pin the fabric strip around the base ring, lining up the drawn marks to the struts. Pull the gathers if needed so it sits tightly around and on top of the stitches on the lampshade.

Make small stitches along the top of the gathered trim, sewing it to the base ring so that the trim covers the stitches of the lining and cover. You can choose to keep this with raw edges or, as with this example, cover the stitches with pre-made bias binding or make your own bias, and attach it with textile glue or small stitches over the top, turning in the ends. *See* the completed trim in Chapter 6.

Rose Trim

In addition, the tube you have made can be fashioned into roses:

The completed rose trim; using a length of a frilled trim, roses can be created by wrapping it around until you have the required size.

This trim has two cut lengths, one of wool tartan and the other a taupe linen.

1. Cut the height as you wish: here it is 5cm for each fabric. Then place the right sides together, and machine them together 2.5mm in from the edges.

2. Turn it over so it is now right sides up, and iron it flat along the length.

3. As above, place running stitch along the raw edges and pull to gather the strip, turning in the cut ends of the fabric strip and slip stitching them.

4. Then fold and curl one end in, and roll it into a circle – the frill will make petal-like edges. Keep going until you have the required-size rose.

5. Turn the rose upside down and make stitches across its base, ensuring each edge is caught in, to avoid unravelling.

6. You can now sew this onto the frame, using small stitches at the back of it, on the lampshade base ring.

TIPS FOR ADDING TRIMS

To get the best results for adding and attaching trims to your lampshades:

- When attaching a braid, you will have cut edges (that tend to unravel a little) – allow 5mm extra to each end of the cut length, which will be folded under. Place a little double-sided tape underneath the 5mm, then fold and stick it down. You will now have two smooth end edges of braid to abut for a neat seam.
- Position all the seams in line with the seams of your lampshades. That way all the workings will be together.
- If using a glue to attach trims, ensure you are using one especially formulated for textiles. For hand sewn lampshades, however, attaching the trims by hand sewing is preferable.
- You may find that some trims arrive with beautiful glass beads but they are attached to a skimpy ribbon. Attach the trim and then add a bias binding as well over the top of the ribbon.
- When stitching trims to the lampshade base ring, ensure they are placed over the stitches of the lampshade cover itself – these will be just on the front of the ring and therefore you will not go through to the inside of it.
- If using bias binding, attach it by stretching it little by little as you go around – it will hug the curves of the frame for a perfect fit. This is important especially if the frame has a scalloped base ring.

Follow these steps to make the rose trim, choosing whether to have the pattern inside the petals or on the outside.

APPENDIX

LAMPSHADE GUIDANCE NOTES

The chapters in the book have information on the materials and fabrics needed, and the methods required to make many different styles of lampshades. However, the following pointers act as an overall guide on lampshades.

Lampshade Sizes and Measurements

Lampshade sizes refer to the base ring diameter, so one that has a 30cm measurement across the lamp base (its diameter measurement), is called a 30cm lampshade. In traditional lampshade making, the full frames are often still named using imperial units, so one with a 30cm base diameter is called a 12in frame.

Choosing Your Lampshade Sizes

To choose which size lampshade you would like to make for a table lamp base, there is nothing better than being able to try different sizes on in advance to see visually which fit best together. This way you will see instantly if the proportions work. However, this is often not possible, and so it may be helpful to follow these key points:

- The diameter of the base ring of the lampshade should match the height of the lamp base.
- The height of the lampshade should be around two thirds of the height of the lamp base.
- The lamp base may have large fittings – ensure the lampshade will sit low enough to hide these.

For standard or floor lamps, lampshades with a 45cm base ring diameter or over are recommended, but this does depend on the size of the lamp stand. Ceiling lampshades

Although there are no hard and fast rules, it is best for a lampshade to work proportionally with its base. Lampshade made by Jane Warren using paper by Pink Artisans.

can be as large as you wish but do check out the ceiling fittings if you decide on a heavy-framed lampshade. It is more appealing to look up into gathers, colourful fabric, or an interesting design than a bright white lining on large ceiling lampshades. Therefore plan to use a decorative inner to the lampshade, and consider its role – whether it is to brighten the room (task lighting) or be a decorative item as part of the room's design.

Fire Retardancy

Most light bulbs used are now LED. These are far more energy efficient and are cool to the touch. Lampshades will therefore not get scorched as they once did. However, it is still a good idea to protect your work; for peace of mind after making a soft hand sewn lampshade, place it into a cardboard box, take it outside, and spray the lining with a water-based fire-proofing spray.

The laminate material used to make hard lampshades is fire retardant – it has been tested in the Lighting Association Laboratories and has passed the glow wire test. Any fabric or paper that is laminated to it will become fire resistant too – even when adding paper or fabric on the inside of the lampshade.

Caring for Your Lampshades

Clean your lampshades by using a soft brush to remove dust, both inside and outside. Use a soft cloth to clean any trims and the light bulb. It is best not to position your lampshade where it receives full sun during the day, as the fabric will fade, and silk, for example, will rot.

Which Lampshade for Which Position?

- For large ceiling lampshades, consider having a patterned fabric or paper inside. This is far more interesting than looking up into a white space.
- For low-down lampshades, perhaps positioned on a side table, it may be better not to use a duplex fitting – otherwise there will be a lot of metalware on show.
- For hall tables or small bedside tables, consider making oval lampshades – they are shallower and therefore take up less space.
- The colour on the inside of the lampshade will be the light emitted into the room, so for a reading lamp, you may prefer to have a white interior as opposed to a decorative colourful fabric inside.

Lighting brings your rooms to life, adding warmth, atmosphere, and decorated design. Enjoy making your lampshades – it is a wonderful skill to have.

Lampshades add decorative design details to a room's decor. Adding a pop of yellow to this blue room, this lampshade was made by Andrea Lord of Bohemia Interiors.

GLOSSARY

Base ring – the ring situated at the bottom of the lampshade frame or the lampshade

Bias or the cross – the 45-degree or diagonal angle on fabric, running across the warp and weft threads, giving stretch to the fabric

Binding tape – a woven tape used for binding full lampshade frames, sometimes called India tape

Bodkin – a large, blunt needle used for pulling ribbon, cord, or elastic through a hem

Channel – a narrow hem created to pull a length of elastic or ribbon through to then pull and gather up

Cone or coolie lampshade – one with a much smaller top ring than base ring, usually one third of the measurement

Diffuser – a disc, usually positioned in the base of the lampshade, that diffuses light into the room, and hides the bulb

Double-sided tape (DST) – used to make hard lampshades as well as attaching trims

Duplex – a fitting in the ring or frame that allows the lampshade to be used either with a lamp stand (using a shade carrier) or with a ceiling pendant (using a spider fitting)

Empire – a shape of lampshade where the top ring is usually half the size of the base ring

Face down – the pattern on the fabric will be placed down, that is, away from you

Face up – the pattern on the fabric will be placed up, that is, towards you

French drum – a shape of lampshade where the top ring is smaller than the base ring but only marginally so

Gimbal fittings – the metal 'arms' that connect the light fitting to the frame or ring set; in hard lampshades, this is the utility ring; in soft lampshade making they may be attached to either the top or base rings of the frame

Grain line – the direction of the woven threads of the fabric, running parallel to the selvedge (the warp threads)

Handling allowance – extra fabric to hold onto in order to position the main fabric taut and in place (sometimes called 'working allowance')

Hem – a turned-under and sewn edge on fabric to hide raw edges

Interlining – a lining that sits on the outside of the frame, under the main outer cover, sometimes called an external lining or undercover

Kiss cuts – the scores made in the laminate panel's horizontal edges 15mm from the edges, supplied in hard lampshade-making kits

Laminate – the heat-resistant material used for making hard lampshades

Light fitting – either in a utility ring (hard lampshades) or full frame, this is used to connect the lampshade to the lamp holder, either on a lamp base or ceiling/pendant

Needle grabbers/grippers – tools to help grip the needle when pulling it through fabric

Pattern repeat – the measured distance between the repeating pattern on fabric both vertically and horizontally

Pi – the Greek symbol for the number used in the mathematical formula for finding the circumference measurement from the diameter measurement; rounded to 3.14 in this book

Raw edge – the cut edge of fabric, which can fray

Railroad – when fabric or paper is turned on its side so the height becomes the width (that is, turned 90 degrees), so the selvedge is horizontal instead of vertical

Right side – the side of the fabric that the pattern is printed on, and facing up or towards you (same as 'face up')

Score line – using an awl or other tool to score lines in laminate or paper for accurate folding

Seam allowance – the extra amount of fabric required to make seams

Seam ripper/unstitcher – a useful tool should you wish to unpick stitches

Sectional – where fabric is sewn onto a frame in sections

Selvedge – the self-finished vertical edges of fabric, running parallel to the warp threads

Semi-gathered/pleated lining – lining that is fitted around the base ring but gathered or pleated around the top ring (on an empire or French drum lampshade frame)

Shade carrier – an adaptor used with a lampshade's duplex fitting, for lamp bases or lamp stands

Spider fitting – an adaptor used with a lampshade's duplex fitting to suspend it from a ceiling

The straight – the 'straight of grain' of the fabric, that is, the fabric is used with the vertical and horizontal (warp and weft) in the correct position

Streetly stitch – sometimes called 'lampshade stitch'; the interconnecting stitch used for sewing covers onto a bound lampshade frame

Struts – the vertical metal rods that connect the top and base rings in full lampshade frames

Tailor's tacks – loose, temporary, hand sewn stitches, used for marking precise points on your fabric

Template – a drawn shape or pattern created so that it can be traced around on fabric or laminate, and can then be reused

Top ring – the top of the lampshade, either of a frame for soft lampshades or a single ring for hard lampshades

Warp and weft – the names given to the direction of the threads used to weave fabrics, the warp running vertically and the weft running horizontally

Working strut – this is the key strut on a soft lampshade frame, where the binding starts/ends, and the seams are positioned

Wrong side – this is the opposite of the 'right side' of the fabric, that is, it does not have the pattern printed on it (same as 'face down')

SUPPLIERS

Lampshade Making Materials
Dannells
www.dannells.com
Manufacturer of kits, laminates, components, frames, and sundry lampshade-making materials

Frames
Richard Meredith
meredith145@btinternet.com
Independent bespoke frame maker, supplier of stock frames for soft and hard lampshade making

Lampshade Binding Tape
Richard Meredith – as above

Lamp Bases
Dannells, as above, supplies a range of unpainted lamp bases, complete with flex, and are fully tested

Cambridge House
www.cambridgehousedesign.com
Beautiful hand-decorated lampshade bases

Fabrics
James Hare
www.james-hare.com
Supplier of a huge range of silks, faux silks, linens, and wools, as well as trims

Pongees
www.pongees.co.uk
Specialist supplier of fine silks – plain dyed, embroidered, and jacquard

Haines
https://hainescollection.co.uk
A fabric resale website, whose mission is to reduce waste in the interiors industry

Cloth House
www.clothhouse.com
Supplier of variety of fine fabrics from around the world

Clothkits
www.clothkits.co.uk
Supplier of a variety of fine fabrics – including Liberty, trims, and kits

Molly Mahon
https://mollymahon.com
Beautiful block-printed fabrics

Etsy
www.etsy.com
A mix of designers' own fabric and stock items – perfect for block prints, linens, and so on

Lining Fabrics

Lycra
DSI London
www.dsi-london.com
The 1203 Lycra is perfect for stretch balloon linings

Crêpe Satin
James Hare – as above
Pongees – as above

Linens
Cloth House – as above

Papers
Cambridge Imprint
www.cambridgeimprint.co.uk
Cambridge-based paper-making company, designing and printing high-quality, colourful, patterned paper

Jemma Lewis Marbling & Design
www.jemmamarbling.com
A comprehensive range of colourful hand-marbled papers, offering off-the-shelf and bespoke designs

Lavender Home
www.lavenderhome.co.uk
Japanese *yuzen* and *washi* papers, some in larger sizes perfect for lampshades

Maiden Marbling
www.maidenmarbling.com
Hand-marbled papers, including bespoke larger sizes for lampshade making

Pink Artisans
Instagram: @pinkartisans
Beautiful hand-marbled and printed papers from Jaipur

Wanderlust Paper Co.
www.wanderlustpaper.co
Papers printed from original artworks, lovely for lampshades

Trims

Barnett Lawson Trimmings
https://barnettlawson.co.uk
Quality fringes, feathers, and braid supplier

Petershams
www.petershams.com
Petersham ribbon in various widths

V V Rouleaux
www.vvrouleaux.com
Extensive range of trims, from quality ribbons to fringes, braids, and tassels

Bespoke Handmade Trims

Jessica Light
www.jessicalightshop.com
All tassels, tie-backs, and trims are hand-woven and handmade to order

Haberdashery

Threads
William Gee
www.williamgee.co.uk
Haberdashers and suppliers of Terko satin thread and other haberdashery

Needles
John James
www.jjneedles.com
Darners and curved needles

Needle Grabbers and Grippers
Silicone needle grabbers by Prym, fit onto thumb and finger to grip needle – various online stores and shops

Simplicity EZ Quilting Needle Gripper – looks like scissors but has gripper teeth to take hold of needle – various online stores and shops

Pins

Jaycotts
https://jaycotts.co.uk
For applique pins, dressmaker pins, tailor's chalk, and other haberdashery
Lils or sequin pins – various online suppliers

Textile glues

Gütermann
https://consumer.guetermann.com/en
Creativ HT2 textile glue – contact them for stockists, or you can find in various online stores and in shops

Groves Ltd
www.grovesltd.co.uk
Original Hi-Tack All Purpose glue – contact them for stockists, or you can find in various online stores and in shops

Grid rules and Cutting Mats

Creative Grids
www.creativegrids.com
World leaders in non-slip grids, which come in both metric and imperial sizes, and have the bias line printed; cutting mats and rotary cutters

Paint

PlastiKote
https://plasti-kote.co.uk
Spray paints in a variety of colours and finishes, plus primers from the ColorMatic range – perfect for repurposing lampshade ring sets and frames

Suppliers for Accordion Pleated Lampshade Materials

Laminate
Dannells – as above
Choose the 'less rigid' laminate backing

Bone Folders
Shepherds London
www.bookbinding.co.uk
The Teflon folders are more gentle on papers than the bone folders; also supplies decorative papers

Hole Punches

A 5mm single hole punch – McGill ³⁄₁₆in-4.765mm Punchline series is recommended – various online suppliers

Wooden-Handled Awl

12cm long wooden-handled awl – various online suppliers, including Hobbycraft
www.hobbycraft.co.uk

Bulldog Clips

20mm wide clips – various online suppliers, including Hobbycraft – as above

Flame Retardant Sprays

Dannells – as above

Block and Screen Printing Supplies

Handprinted
www.handprinted.co.uk
Sells large range of materials for printing, plus studio-based workshops

Suppliers for Liberty Little Lights

Fabric – Clothkits – as above

Cups – 10oz, paper, various suppliers online

Decoupage glue – Mod Podge Matte Finish – various suppliers online including art shops

Brushes – small – from art shops or various suppliers online

Lights – battery-operated LED lights, strings of ten or more, various online suppliers; two AA batteries are required

Trims – V V Rouleaux – as above

3mm double-sided tape – Dannells – as above

CONTRIBUTORS

More information on the author, Jane Warren, as well as her designs and workshops, can be found at:

www.thelampshadeloft.co.uk
Instagram: @thelampshadeloft

Many thanks to the contributors whose photographs of their wonderful work appear in the book:

Alison Bick Designs
https://alisonbick.co.uk
Instagram: @alisonbickdesigns
Photographs of Alison Bick's work are by Anya Rice and Liz Kaye

Anna Vojtisek
www.annavojtisek.com
Instagram @annavojtisek

The Bespoke Boutique
www.thebespokeboutique.co.uk
Instagram: @thebespokeboutique

Bohemia Interiors
www.bohemia-interiors.co.uk
Instagram: @bohemiainteriors

Bridget Arnold
www.bridgetarnold.co.uk
Instagram: @bridget9696

Caitlin Warren
www.caitlinisobelwarren.com
Instagram: @caitlinisobelwarren

Candid Owl Limited
https://candidowl.com
Instagram: @candidowl

Charlotte Tøt Jensen – Shades by DK
https://shadesby.dk
Instagram: @igenibrug and @shades.by.igenibrug

Detola & Geek
https://detolaandgeek.com
Instagram: @detolaandgeek

Fringe Handcrafted Lampshades
Fringehandcraftedlampshades@gmail.com
Instagram: @fringe_handcrafted_lampshades

Glow Lampshades
www.glowlampshades.co.uk
Instagram: @glowlampshades

Jane Ellison Textiles
www.janeellisontextiles.com
Instagram: @janellisontextiles

Jennifer Fraser Lampshades
www.jenniferfraserlampshades.com
Instagram: @jenniferfraserlampshades

Jessica Light
www.jessicalightshop.com
Instagram: @jessica_light_

Light Owl
https://lightowl.co.uk
Instagram: @lightowluk

Light Stylist
https://lightstylist.co.uk
Instagram: @lightstylist_uk

Melodi Horne
www.melodihorne.com
Instagram: @melodihorne
Photograph by Tim Beddow

Mono Handmade
www.monohandmade.co.uk
Instagram: @monohandmadelampshades

Ooh La La Lampshades
www.oohlalalampshades.co.uk
Instagram: @oohlala_lampshades

Parlour Made
https://parlourmadeuk.com
Instagram: @parlourmadeuk
Photographs of Marie Monro's work are by Johnny Gallagher

Revill, Revill Lampshades
www.revillrevillshop.com
Instagram: @revillrevilllampshades

Rock Paper Scissors Shades
www.rockpaperscissorsshades.co.uk
Instagram: @rockpaperscissorsshades

Ryan Coombes Designs
www.ryancoombesdesigns.co.uk
Instagram: @ryan_coombes_designs

Shady and the Lamp
https://shadyandthelamp.ie
Instagram: @shadyandthelamp

Silkworm and Cottontails
www.silkwormandcottontails.com
Instagram: @silkworm_and_cottontails

Sophia Frances Studio
www.sophiafrances.com
Instagram: @sophiafrances_studio

Wyre & Gimble
Amanda Wheatland
Instagram: @wyreandgimble

INDEX

First published in 2024 by
The Crowood Press Ltd
Ramsbury, Marlborough
Wiltshire SN8 2HR

enquiries@crowood.com
www.crowood.com

British Library Cataloguing-in-Publication Data

A catalogue record for this book is available from the
British Library.

ISBN 978 0 7198 4334 1

Jane Warren has asserted their right under the Copyright,
Designs and Patents Act 1988 to be identified as the
author of this work.

Cover design by Susan Richards
Diagrams by Maria Pulley
Instagram @maria.pulley
Further diagrams by Ian J. Fleming

Dedication
This book is dedicated to my lovely and creative
daughter, Caitlin – you inspire me every day – I love you
more than cats, the stars, and lampshades. And my love
to you, Ian – you have unstintingly supported me with
endless cups of tea, editorial help, and love – thank you.

Graphic design and typesetting by Peggy & Co. Design
Printed and bound in India by Thomson Press India Ltd.

Acknowledgements

I would like to thank the following who have kindly
supported me in the writing of this book: James Dannell
(Dannells) – for your advice and wonderful materials
(including the lampshade-making kits used in this book)
and for permission to re-draw some of your diagrams – and
for your endless good humour! Richard Meredith – for
frames supplied to make the soft lampshades and your
excellent bespoke frame-making skills.

James Hare – for the crêpe-backed satin used to make
the gathered linings; Pongees for the dupion silk used to
make the pleated lampshades; V V Rouleaux for the generous supply of trimmings, perfect for lampshades; Barnett
Lawson Trimmings – for the long and silky fringe trim used
to make the Tiffany lampshade; PlastiKote – for a supply
of primer and paints, for repurposing the vintage and used
lampshade frames; Creative Grids (UK) – for the top quality
non-slip rulers – perfect for lampshade making of all types.

For allowing me to share images of their lampshades I
have made for them, thank you to: Helen Mackenzie, The
Curtain Co – the double-sided lampshade made using
wallpaper by Zoffany; Claudine Purnell – the pendant
lampshade was made for Claudine's library room, using
Penguin Library Wallpaper by Osborne & Little; Lucy
Quick – the oversized lampshade in design by Josef Frank,
and lined with sunshine yellow linen.

Thank you to the following whose paper I have used
to make some of the lampshades in the book: Cambridge
Imprint; Jemma Lewis Marbling; Lavender Home; Maiden
Marbling; Molly Mahon; Pink Artisans; Wanderlust
Paper Co.

Thank you also to Kay Mawer of Clothkits and your
team (especially Karen and Rachel) – for spreading the
lampshade love by hosting the best run workshops; Maria
Pulley (Instagram: @maria.pulley) – for your superb drawing skills, thank you Special thanks go to Elizabeth Pegg, an
ace lampshade maker – thank you for the skill swaps and
friendship over the years.